Have a special Xmas
and wonderful 2014

lox
Dad, Suzie
  x

TASCHEN

365

A YEAR IN PICTURES

DAY BY DAY

MOVIE ICONS

TASCHEN

"Here we are now — entertain us!"

Moulin Rouge!

Baz Luhrmann, 2001
Nicole Kidman, Richard Roxburgh

"All I can do is be me.
Whoever that is."

I'm Not There

Todd Haynes, 2007
Cate Blanchett

Pola Negri (1897)
John Sturges (1910)
Sergio Leone (1929)
Mel Gibson (1956)

Once Upon a Time in America

Es war einmal in Amerika /
Il était une fois en Amérique
Sergio Leone, 1983

All That Heaven Allows

Was der Himmel erlaubt / Tout ce que le ciel permet
Douglas Sirk, 1955
Rock Hudson, Jane Wyman

Robert Duvall (1931)
Hayao Miyazaki (1941)
Diane Keaton (1946)

"I smell something...
a human!"

Hayao Miyazaki

Spirited Away

Chihiros Reise ins Zauberland / Le Voyage de Chihiro
Hayao Miyazaki, 2001
Chihiro

The English Patient

Der englische Patient / Le Patient anglais
Anthony Minghella, 1996
Ralph Fiennes

Nicolas Cage (1964)
Jeremy Renner (1971)

"This is a snakeskin jacket! And for me it's a symbol of my individuality, and my belief in personal freedom!"

Sailor (Nicolas Cage)

Wild at Heart

*Wild at Heart – Die Geschichte
von Sailor und Lula / Sailor et Lula*
David Lynch, 1990
Nicolas Cage

Jailhouse Rock

Rhythmus hinter Gittern /
Le Rock du bagne
Richard Thorpe, 1957
Elvis Presley

Metropolis

Fritz Lang, 1926
Rudolf Klein-Rogge

Easy Rider

Dennis Hopper, 1969
Dennis Hopper, Henry Fonda

Bernard Blier (1916)
Rod Taylor (1930)
Christine Kaufmann (1945)

"God put you in my path and I aim to cure you of your wicked ways."

Lazarus (Samuel L. Jackson) to Rae (Christina Ricci)

Black Snake Moan

Craig Brewer, 2006
Christina Ricci

Luise Rainer (1910)
Mary Harron (1953)
John Lasseter (1957)

"In space, no one can hear you clean."

WALL·E

WALL·E – Der Letzte räumt die Erde auf
Andrew Stanton, 2008
WALL·E

Every Man for Himself

Rette sich, wer kann (Das Leben) /
Sauve qui peut (la vie)
Jean-Luc Godard, 1980
Isabelle Huppert

Faye Dunaway (1941)
Steven Soderbergh (1963)

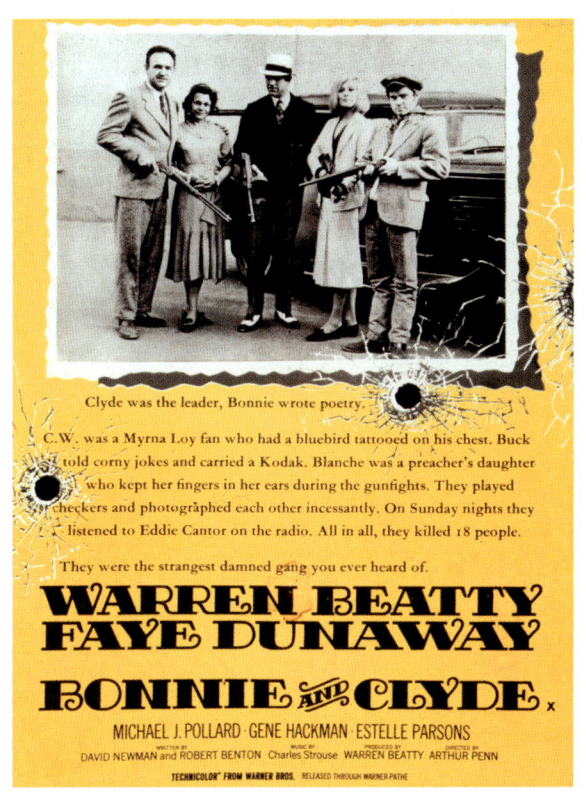

Bonnie and Clyde

Bonnie und Clyde / Bonnie et Clyde
Arthur Penn, 1967
Faye Dunaway

Planes, Trains & Automobiles

Ein Ticket für Zwei / Un ticket pour deux
John Hughes, 1987
Steve Martin, John Candy

3 facher Saltomortale vom Trapez in die Hände des Fängers. Einzig in der Welt.

Karl Freund (1890)
John Carpenter (1948)

"Impressionistic lighting, lingering expressionist imagery, and giddily mobile camerawork are all pushed to unprecedented extremes, like Murnau on speed."

Time Out Film Guide

Jealousy

Varieté / Variétés
E.A. Dupont, 1925
Warwick Ward, Lya De Putti

Jim Carrey (1962)
Lukas Moodysson (1969)

"Sometimes I feel that Swedish films should get less money. Because we don't make very good films, so why should we make more films?"

Lukas Moodysson

On the set of
Together

Zusammen!
Lukas Moodysson, 2000

"It's the best film I've ever done. It's a picture that just picks you up and sends you crashing against the rocks. You feel everything and just crawl out of the theater."

Burt Reynolds

Deliverance

Beim Sterben ist jeder der Erste / Délivrance
John Boorman, 1972
Jon Voight, Ned Beatty

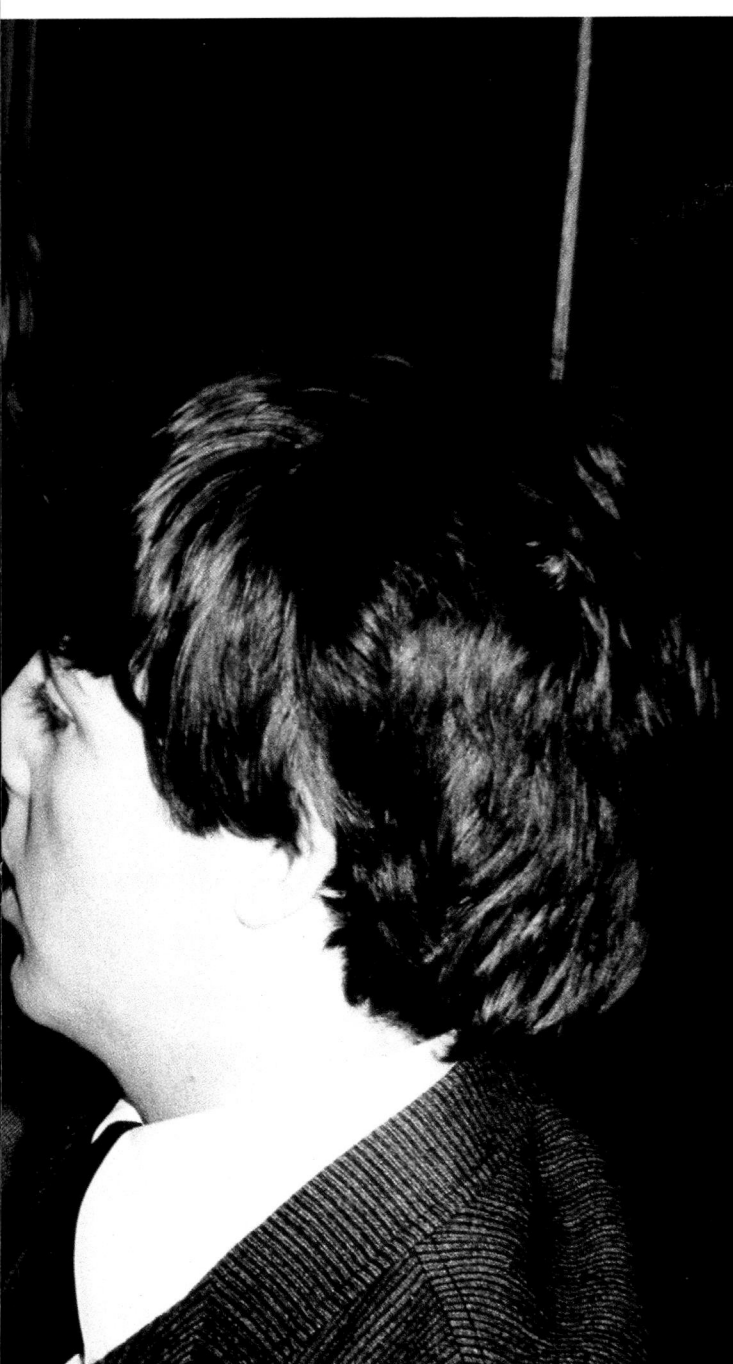

Lilian Harvey (1906)
Tippi Hedren (1930)
Richard Lester (1932)

A Hard Day's Night

Yeah Yeah Yeah /
Quatre garçons dans le vent
Richard Lester, 1964
George Harrison, Ringo Starr,
Paul McCartney

Federico Fellini (1920)
David Lynch (1946)

Lost Highway

David Lynch, 1996
Patricia Arquette

JANUARY 21

Telly Savalas (1922)
Paul Scofield (1922)
Geena Davis (1956)
Marie Trintignant (1962)

Thelma & Louise

Ridley Scott, 1991
Susan Sarandon, Geena Davis

> **"Griffith assembled and perfected the early discoveries of film language, and his cinematic techniques that have influenced the visual strategies of virtually every film made since."**

Roger Ebert

The Birth of a Nation

Die Geburt einer Nation / Naissance d'une nation
D.W. Griffith, 1915
Lillian Gish

Randolph Scott (1898)
Sergei Eisenstein (1898)
Jeanne Moreau (1928)

Ivan the Terrible, Part II

Iwan der Schreckliche, Teil II / Ivan le Terrible II
Sergei Eisenstein, 1944/58
Pavel Kadotchnikov

JANUARY 24

Ernest Borgnine (1917)
Michel Serrault (1928)
John Belushi (1949)
Daniel Auteuil (1950)
Nastassja Kinski (1961)

Deadly Circuit

Das Auge / Mortelle randonnée
Claude Miller, 1982
Michel Serrault

Carlos

Carlos – Der Schakal / Carlos
Olivier Assayas, 2010
Édgar Ramírez

Paul Newman (1925)
Nuri Bilge Ceylan (1959)

"What we've got here ... is failure to communicate."

Luke (Paul Newman)

Cool Hand Luke

Der Unbeugsame / Luke la main froide
Stuart Rosenberg, 1967
Paul Newman

Sin City

Robert Rodriguez, Frank Miller, 2005
Devon Aoki

Ernst Lubitsch (1892)
Elijah Wood (1981)

"One ring to rule them all, one ring to find them, one ring to bring them all and in the darkness bind them."

The inscription upon the ring

The Lord of the Rings: The Two Towers

Der Herr der Ringe – Die zwei Türme /
Le Seigneur des anneaux – Les deux tours
Peter Jackson, 2002
Elijah Wood

W. C. Fields (1880)
Paddy Chayefsky (1923)

"Do you have any idea how crazy you are?"

Carson Wells (Woody Harrelson)

No Country for Old Men

Ethan Coen, Joel Coen, 2007
Javier Bardem

Dorothy Malone (1925)
Gene Hackman (1930)
Vanessa Redgrave (1937)
Christian Bale (1974)

The Big Sleep

Tote schlafen fest / Le Grand Sommeil
Howard Hawks, 1946
Lauren Bacall, Humphrey Bogart

The Emperor Waltz

Ich küsse Ihre Hand, Madame /
La Valse de l'empereur
Billy Wilder, 1948
Bing Crosby

"You can go back and have what you like of it, if you can remember."

Huw Morgan (Roddy McDowall)

How Green Was My Valley

So grün war mein Tal / Qu'elle était verte ma vallée
John Ford, 1941
Roddy McDowall

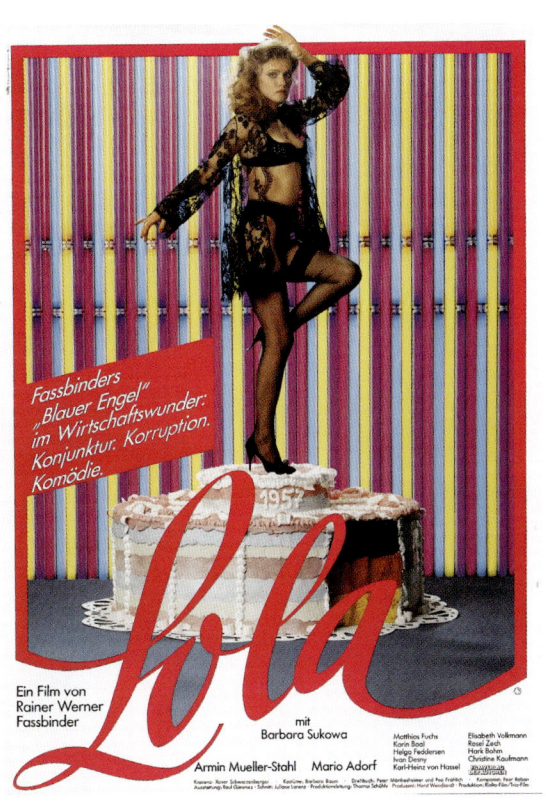

Lola

Lola, une femme allemande
Rainer Werner Fassbinder, 1981
Mario Adorf, Barbara Sukowa

"One shot is what it's all about. A deer has to be taken with one shot."

Michael (Robert De Niro)

The Deer Hunter

Die durch die Hölle gehen / Voyage au bout de l'enfer
Michael Cimino, 1978
Robert De Niro, Christopher Walken

Ida Lupino (1918)
George Romero (1940)

"As gangster pictures go, this one has everything—speed, excitement, suspense and that ennobling suggestion of futility which makes for irony and pity. Mr. Bogart plays the leading role with a perfection of hard-boiled vitality, and Ida Lupino ... [is] impressive as the adoring moll."

The New York Times

High Sierra

Entscheidung in der Sierra / La Grande Évasion
Raoul Walsh, 1941
Humphrey Bogart, Ida Lupino

Manhunter

Blutmond / Le Sixième sens
Michael Mann, 1986
Tom Noonan

Amores perros

Amours chiennes
Alejandro González Iñárritu, 2000
Gael García Bernal

Héctor Babenco (1946)
James Spader (1960)

"Every day I am compelled to make things, in whatever medium. I do it because I'm totally captivated by other people and their lives."

Miranda July

Me and You and Everyone We Know

Ich und du und alle die wir kennen /
Moi, toi et tous les autres
Miranda July, 2004
Miranda July

Lana Turner (1921)
Jack Lemmon (1925)
James Dean (1931)

"James Dean was so cool in the film that guys ached to be him and spent hours training their hair into messy pompadours."

San Francisco Chronicle

Rebel Without a Cause

… denn sie wissen nicht, was sie tun / La Fureur de vivre
Nicholas Ray, 1955
James Dean

Joe Pesci (1943)
Zhang Ziyi (1979)

GoodFellas

*GoodFellas – Drei Jahrzehnte in der
Mafia / Les Affranchis*
Martin Scorsese, 1990
Joe Pesci, Ray Liotta

FEBRUARY 10

Bertolt Brecht (1898)
Robert Wagner (1930)
Michael Apted (1941)
Laura Dern (1967)

On the set of
Cheyenne Autumn

Cheyenne / Les Cheyennes
John Ford, 1964

All About Eve

Alles über Eva / Ève
Joseph L. Mankiewicz, 1950
Gary Merrill, Bette Davis

"I'm an old broken-down piece of meat, and I deserve to be all alone."

Randy "The Ram" Robinson (Mickey Rourke)

The Wrestler

Darren Aronofsky, 2008
Mickey Rourke

Vertigo

Vertigo – Aus dem Reich der Toten /
Sueurs froides
Alfred Hitchcock, 1958
James Stewart, Kim Novak

Thelma Ritter (1902)
Alexander Kluge (1932)
Alan Parker (1944)

"I wonder if I know what you mean ..."

Phyllis (Barbara Stanwyck)

Double Indemnity

Frau ohne Gewissen / Assurance sur la mort
Billy Wilder, 1944
Barbara Stanwyck

Look Back in Anger

Blick zurück im Zorn / Les Corps sauvages
Tony Richardson, 1959
Richard Burton, Claire Bloom

John Schlesinger (1926)

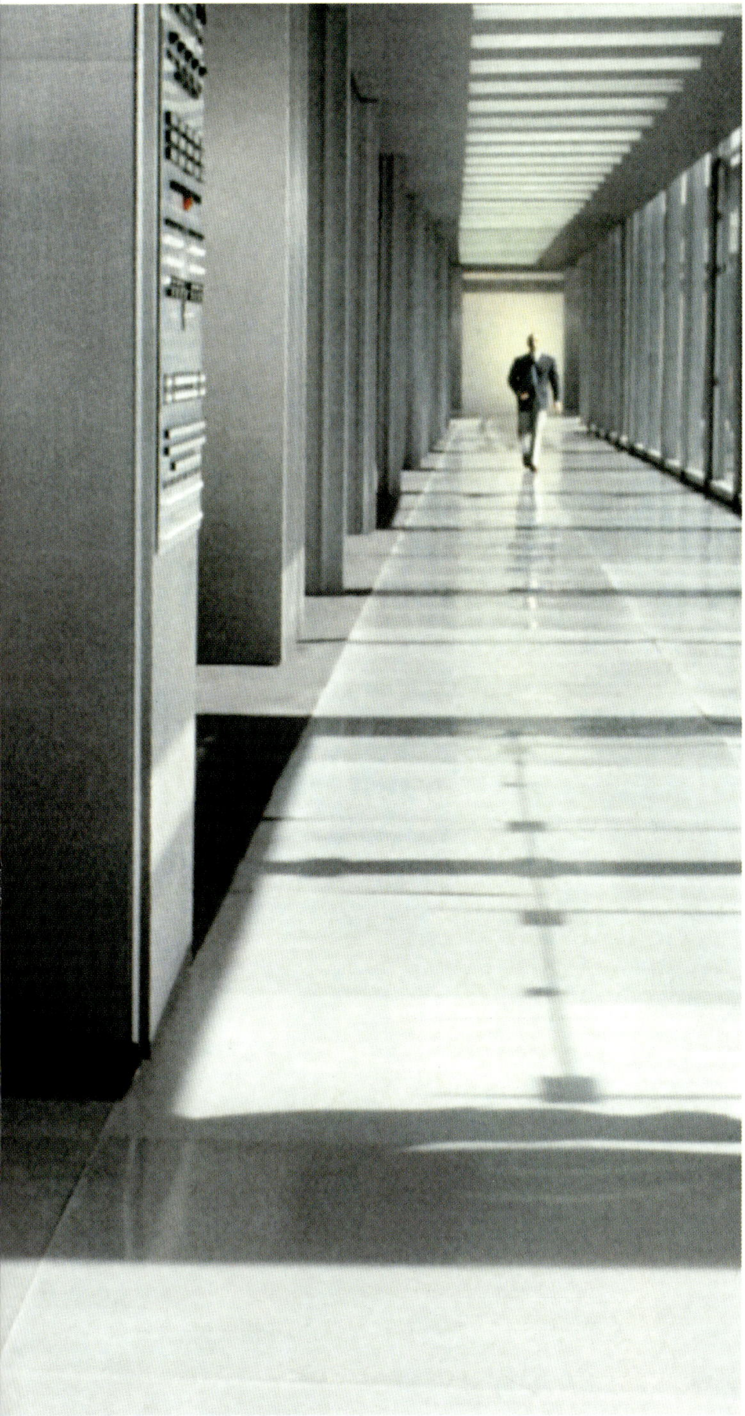

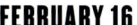

Playtime

Tatis herrliche Zeiten
Jacques Tati, 1967
Jacques Tati

"The sex in this film is far from explicit, though it features geometric formations that may be better suited for Kama Sutra students, or at least the limber. What's explicit here is ravenous passion and the depiction of desire as a creating, destroying force that invades the very flesh. It's terribly French."

The New York Times

The Last Mistress

Die letzte Mätresse / Une vieille maîtresse
Catherine Breillat, 2007
Fu'ad Aït Aattou, Asia Argento

"Why the fuck didn't you tell us somebody was in the bathroom?"

Vincent Vega (John Travolta)

Pulp Fiction

Quentin Tarantino, 1994
John Travolta

Lee Marvin (1924)
Benicio Del Toro (1967)

"One of the main themes is certainly greed. That's a human emotion that I don't understand. I have experienced it often enough, but I don't understand it."

Steven Soderbergh

Traffic

Steven Soderbergh, 2000
Benicio Del Toro

"The funniest epic vision of America ever to reach the screen."

Pauline Kael

Nashville

Robert Altman, 1975
Geraldine Chaplin

Sam Peckinpah (1925)
Ellen Page (1987)

–"I still have your underwear."
–"I still have your virginity."

Paulie Bleeker (Michael Cera) to Juno MacGuff (Ellen Page)

Juno

Jason Reitman, 2007
Ellen Page

Luis Buñuel (1900)
Giulietta Masina (1921)
Jonathan Demme (1944)
Drew Barrymore (1975)

La Strada

La Strada – Das Lied der Straße / La Strada
Federico Fellini, 1954
Giulietta Masina

The Treasure of the Sierra Madre

Der Schatz der Sierra Madre /
Le Trésor de la Sierra Madre
John Huston, 1947
Humphrey Bogart

The Thomas Crown Affair

Thomas Crown ist nicht zu fassen /
L'Affaire Thomas Crown
Norman Jewison, 1968
Faye Dunaway, Steve McQueen

Zeppo Marx (1901)
Gert Fröbe (1913)
Neil Jordan (1950)

"Such a devil cannot possibly exist."

It Happened in Broad Daylight

Es geschah am hellichten Tag /
Ça s'est passé en plein jour
Ladislao Vajda, 1958
Gert Fröbe

"How'd you like to tussle with Russell?"

The Outlaw

Geächtet / Le Banni
Howard Hughes, 1941/43
Jane Russell, Jack Buetel

Cleopatra

Cléopâtre
Joseph L. Mankiewicz, 1963
Elizabeth Taylor

Vincente Minnelli (1903)
Guy Maddin (1956)

"Back home everyone said I didn't have any talent. They might be saying the same thing over here, but it sounds better in French."

Jerry Mulligan (Gene Kelly)

An American in Paris

Ein Amerikaner in Paris / Un américain à Paris
Vincente Minnelli, 1951
Leslie Caron, Gene Kelly

David Niven (1910)
Ron Howard (1954)
Javier Bardem (1969)

"Why do people have to tell lies?"

Regina Lampert (Audrey Hepburn)

Charade

Stanley Donen, 1963
Audrey Hepburn

Tom Wolfe (1931)
Daniel Craig (1968)

–"Shaken or stirred?"
–"Do I look like I give a damn?"

Bartender (Dusan Pelech) to James Bond (Daniel Craig)

Casino Royale

James Bond 007 – Casino Royale
Martin Campbell, 2006
Daniel Craig

11490-110

Jean Harlow (1911)
George Miller (1945)

"Did anyone ever tell you you had the most beautiful legs in the world?"

Stanislas Kasava (Robert Strauss)

Stalag 17

Billy Wilder, 1953
Harvey Lembeck, Robert Strauss

James Ellroy (1948)

−"Why did you become a cop?"
−"I don't remember."

Ed Exley (Guy Pearce) to Jack Vincennes (Kevin Spacey)

L.A. Confidential

Curtis Hanson, 1997
Kim Basinger

Accattone

Accattone – Wer nie sein Brot mit Tränen aß
Pier Paolo Pasolini, 1961
Silvana Corsini, Franco Citti

Arnold Fanck (1889)
Lou Costello (1906)

"With the first glistening rays of sun that shoot horizontally across the snow, the first work begins, for these 15 minutes deliver the most wonderful images, these unreal 'photographs' in which the snow crystals sparkle a millionfold against the still-dark shadows."

Arnold Fanck

The White Hell of Pitz Palu

Die weiße Hölle vom Piz Palü /
L'Enfer blanc du Pitz Palu
Arnold Fanck, 1929

Heinz Rühmann (1902)
Anna Magnani (1908)
Rachel Weisz (1970)

"Filmmaking is an exercise in paranoia."

Darren Aronofsky

The Fountain

Darren Aronofsky, 2006
Rachel Weisz

Aidan Quinn (1959)
Christiane Paul (1974)

"My father often said that filmmakers were idiots. He didn't see cinema as a true art form. That was the atmosphere I grew up in as a child."

Jacques Audiard

Read My Lips

Lippenbekenntnisse / Sur mes lèvres
Jacques Audiard, 2001
Vincent Cassel, Emmanuelle Devos

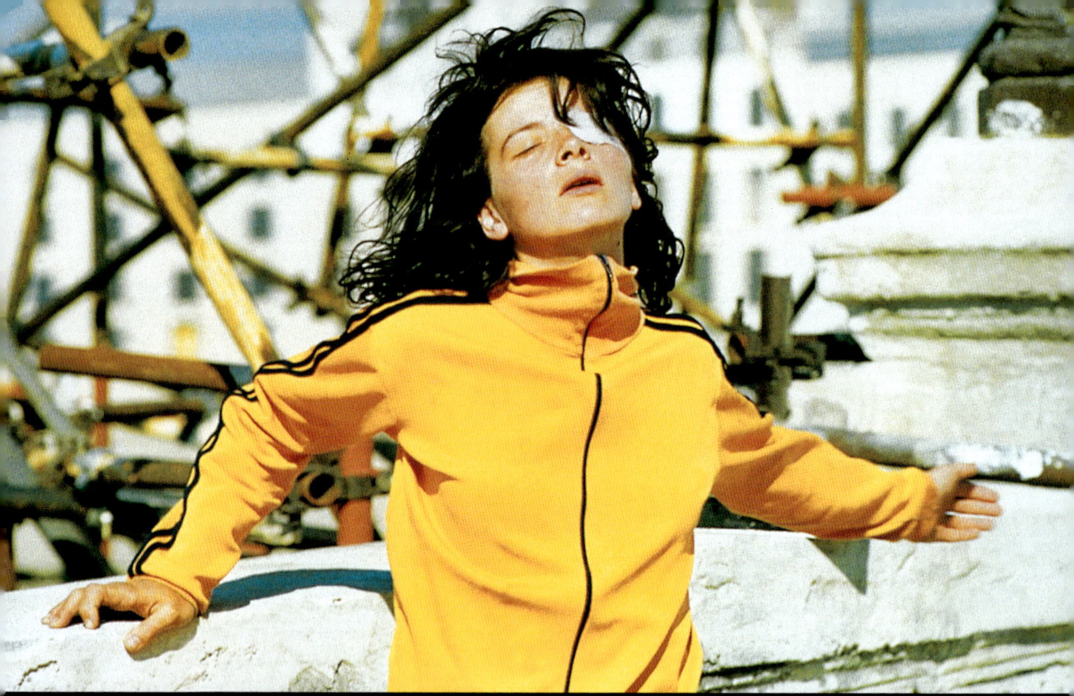

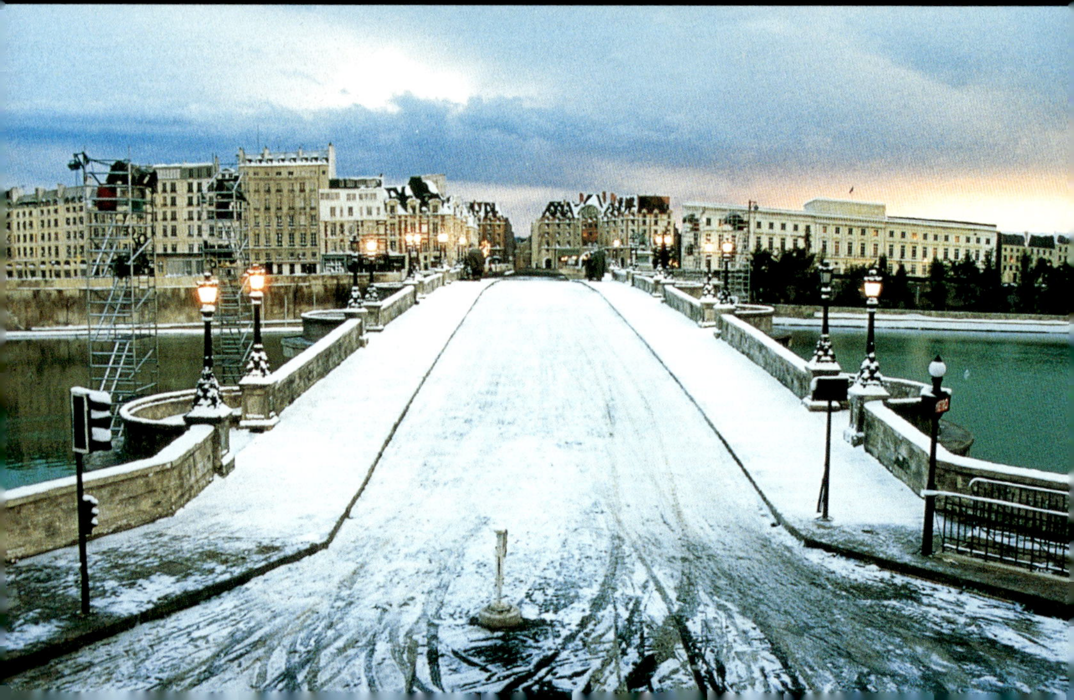

CHRISTIAN FECHNER PRÉSENTE

JULIETTE BINOCHE   DENIS LAVANT

Les Amants du Pont-Neuf

UN FILM DE
LEOS CARAX

Avec KLAUS-MICHAEL GRÜBER dans le rôle de HANS
Producteur délégué BERNARD ARTIGUES
Directeur de la photo JEAN-YVES ESCOFFIER
Décors MICHEL VANDESTIEN
Ingénieur du son HENRI MORELLE
Montage NELLY QUETTIER
Producteurs exécutifs HERVÉ TRUFFAUT - ALBERT PRÉVOST
Directeurs de production CHARLES FERRON - NICOLAS DAGUET
Une coproduction FILMS CHRISTIAN FECHNER - FILMS A2 distribuée par GAUMONT

The Lovers on the Bridge

Die Liebenden von Pont-Neuf /
Les Amants du Pont-Neuf
Leos Carax, 1991
Juliette Binoche

Withnail and I

Withnail et moi
Bruce Robinson, 1986
Paul McGann, Richard E. Grant,
Richard Griffiths

"Not so much an antiwar film as an attack on the military mind."

Pauline Kael

Paths of Glory

Wege zum Ruhm / Les Sentiers de la gloire
Stanley Kubrick, 1957
Kirk Douglas

Cabaret

Bob Fosse, 1972
Liza Minnelli

André Techiné (1943)
William H. Macy (1950)

In a Lonely Place

Ein einsamer Ort / Le Violent
Nicholas Ray, 1950
Humphrey Bogart

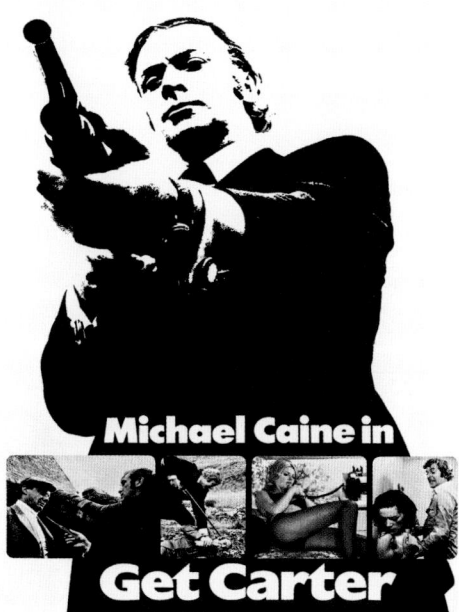

Get Carter

Jack rechnet ab / La Loi du milieu
Mike Hodges, 1971
Michael Caine

"Jeremy Irons plays twin gynecologists in a gut wrencher that's pure Cronenberg."

Rolling Stone

Dead Ringers

Die Unzertrennlichen / Faux-semblants
David Cronenberg, 1988
Jeremy Irons

Jerry Lewis (1926)
Bernardo Bertolucci (1940)
Isabelle Huppert (1953)

**"Two shots of vodka,
a little rum,
some bitters,
a smidgeon of vinegar,
a shot of vermouth,
a shot of gin,
a little brandy,
lemon peel,
orange peel,
a cherry, some more scotch.
Now, mix it nice. Pour it into a tall glass."**

Buddy Love (Jerry Lewis)

The Nutty Professor

Der verrückte Professor / Le Professeur foldingue
Jerry Lewis, 1963
Jerry Lewis

"I don't give a fuck about your war ... or your president."

Snake Plissken (Kurt Russell)

Escape from New York

Die Klapperschlange / New York 1997
John Carpenter, 1981
Kurt Russell

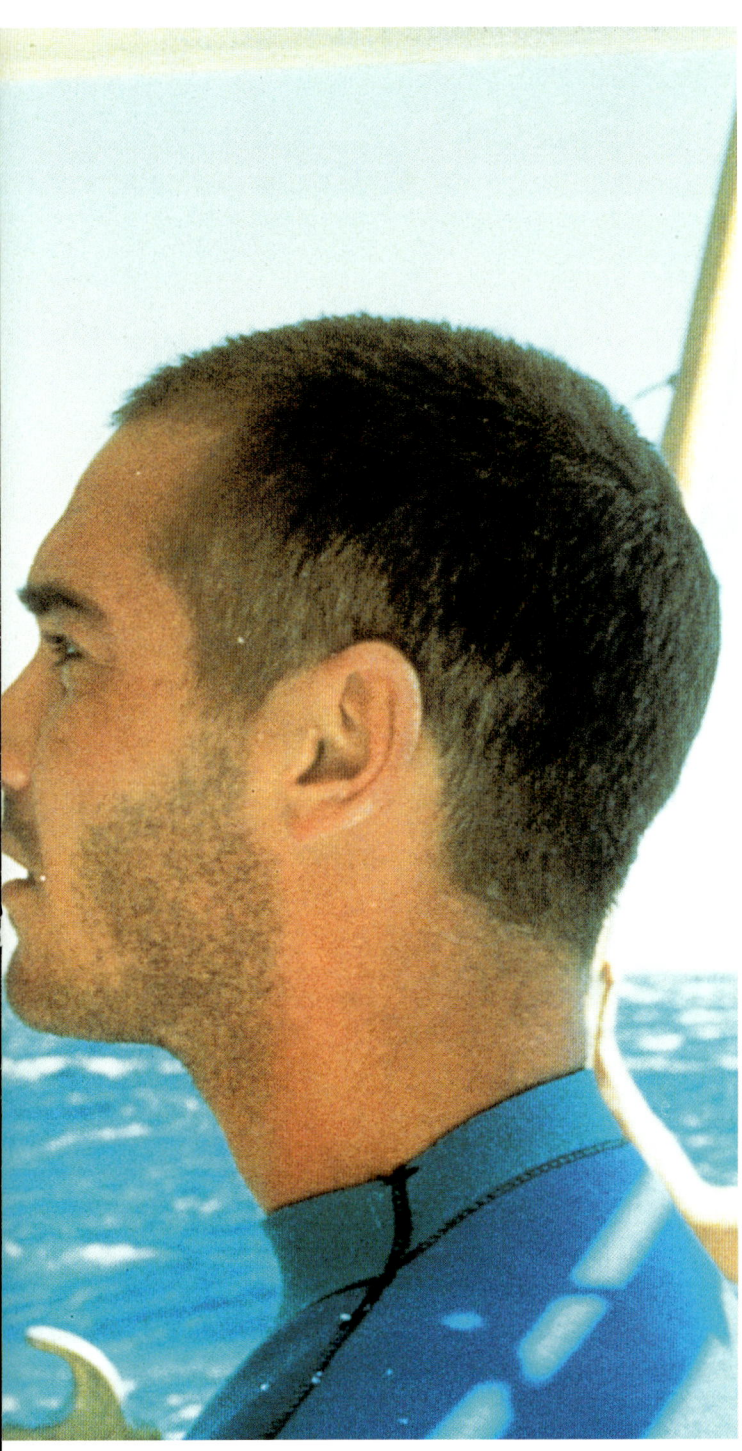

The Big Blue

Im Rausch der Tiefe / Le Grand bleu
Luc Besson, 1988
Jean Reno, Jean-Marc Barr

Ursula Andress (1936)
Glenn Close (1947)
Bruce Willis (1955)

–"You're wonderful."
–"Of course, didn't you know?"

Sam Craig (Spencer Tracy) to Tess Harding (Katharine Hepburn)

Woman of the Year

Die Frau, von der man spricht /
La Femme de l'année
George Stevens, 1941
Spencer Tracy, Katharine Hepburn

The Piano

Das Piano / La Leçon de piano
Jane Campion, 1993
Harvey Keitel, Holly Hunter

The Dark Knight

Le Chevalier noir
Christopher Nolan, 2008
Christian Bale

Chico Marx (1887)
Angelo Badalamenti (1937)
Bruno Ganz (1941)
Reese Witherspoon (1976)

The Postman Always Rings Twice

*Wenn der Postmann zweimal klingelt / Le
facteur sonne toujours deux fois*
Tay Garnett, 1946
John Garfield, Lana Turner

Joan Crawford (1906)
Akira Kurosawa (1910)
Michael Haneke (1942)

The White Ribbon

Das weiße Band – eine deutsche
Kindergeschichte / Le Ruban blanc
Michael Haneke, 2009

The Cincinnati Kid

Cincinnati Kid / Le Kid de Cincinnati
Norman Jewison, 1965
Steve McQueen

"A lot of my work has to do with not allowing
my characters to have an ego in a way
that the stomach doesn't have an ego when
it's wanting to throw up. It just does it."

Matthew Barney

Cremaster 4

Matthew Barney, 1995
Matthew Barney

Nightmare Alley

Der Scharlatan / Le charlatan
Edmund Goulding, 1947
Helen Walker, Tyrone Power

Norma Shearer (1902)
Antonio Banderas (1960)
Cate Shortland (1968)

"Video technology puts filmmaking back in the hands of the people. That's how I learned how to make movies — making movies at home."

Robert Rodriguez

On the set of
Spy Kids 3-D: Game Over

Mission 3D / Spy Kids 3 : Mission 3D
Robert Rodriguez, 2003
Robert Rodriguez, Antonio Banderas

"You can bend the rules plenty once you get to the top, but not while you're trying to get there."

Tess McGill (Melanie Griffith)

Working Girl

Die Waffen der Frauen
Mike Nichols, 1988
Melanie Griffith

Robert Siodmak (1900)
Dustin Hoffman (1937)

"Frankly, you're beginning to smell and for a stud in New York, that's a handicap."

Ratso Rizzo (Dustin Hoffman)

Midnight Cowboy

Asphalt-Cowboy / Macadam Cowboy
John Schlesinger, 1969
Jon Voight, Dustin Hoffman

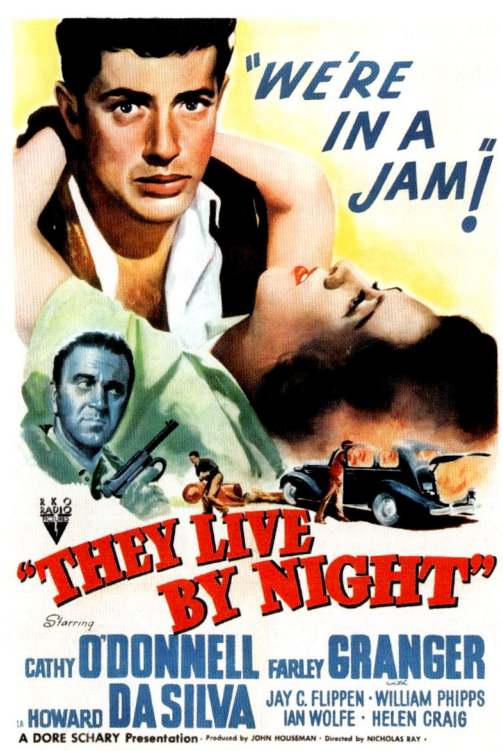

They Live by Night

Nachts unterwegs / Les Amants de la nuit
Nicholas Ray, 1949
Cathy O'Donnell, Farley Granger

"The Original Masterpiece of Revenge, Confrontation and Murder!"

Cape Fear

Ein Köder für die Bestie / Les Nerfs à vif
J. Lee Thompson, 1962
Robert Mitchum

"The best private-eye melodrama ever made."

Life Magazine

The Maltese Falcon

Die Spur des Falken / Le Faucon maltais
John Huston, 1941
Humphrey Bogart

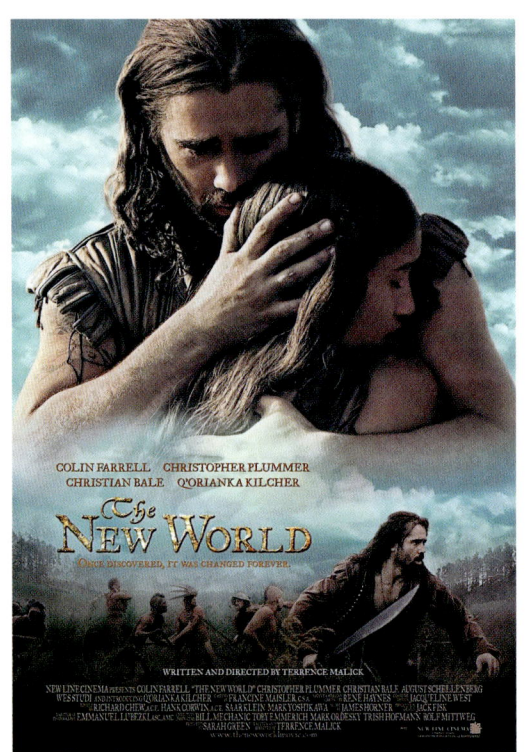

The New World

La Nouveau Monde
Terrence Malick, 2005
Q'orianka Kilcher

Martin Sheen (1940)
Mathieu Kassovitz (1967)

Apocalypse Now

Francis Ford Coppola, 1979
Frederic Forrest, Martin Sheen,
Dennis Hopper

Myrna Loy (1905)
Peter O'Toole (1932)

"The trick, William Potter, is not *minding* that it hurts."

Lawrence (Peter O'Toole)

Lawrence of Arabia

Lawrence von Arabien / Lawrence d'Arabie
David Lean, 1962
Peter O'Toole

AUGUST 1

Giancarlo Giannini (1942)
Sam Mendes (1965)

Revolutionary Road

Zeiten des Aufruhrs / Les Noces rebelles
Sam Mendes, 2008
Leonardo DiCaprio, Kate Winslet

Louis de Funès (1914)
Wesley Snipes (1962)

"A loin of beef — Argentinian, three years old, southern slopes."

Charles Duchemin (Louis de Funès)

The Wing and the Thigh

Brust oder Keule / L'Aile ou la cuisse
Claude Zidi, 1976
Louis de Funès

Arnold Schwarzenegger (1947)
Christopher Nolan (1970)
Hilary Swank (1974)

"I always thought the joy of reading a book is not knowing what happens next."

Leonard Shelby (Guy Pearce)

Memento

Christopher Nolan, 2000
Guy Pearce

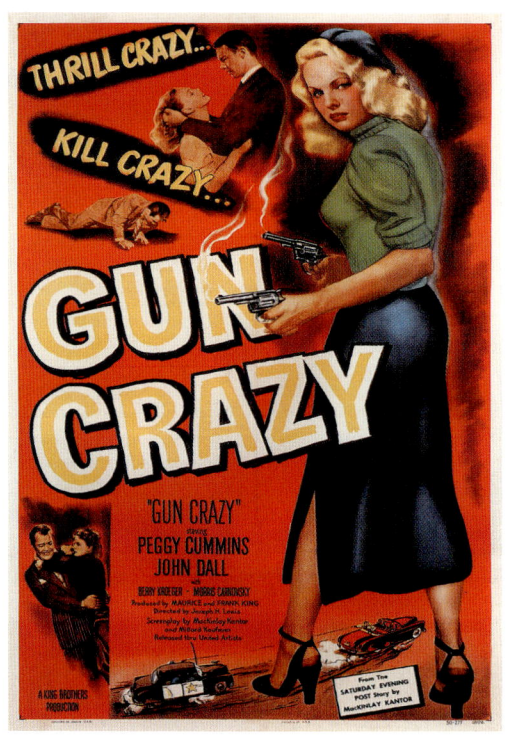

Gun Crazy

Gefährliche Leidenschaft /
Le Démon des armes
Joseph H. Lewis, 1950
Peggy Cummins, John Dall

Notorious

Berüchtigt / Les Enchaînés
Alfred Hitchcock, 1946
Cary Grant, Ingrid Bergman

Donald Crisp (1882)
Jonathan Rhys Meyers (1977)

"Oh, no . . . this is Earth . . . isn't it?"

Thor (Chris Hemsworth)

Thor

Kenneth Branagh, 2011
Chris Hemsworth

Stanley Kubrick (1928)
Helen Mirren (1945)
Kevin Spacey (1959)
Sandra Bullock (1964)

2001: A Space Odyssey

2001: Odyssee im Weltraum /
2001, L'Odyssée de l'espace
Stanley Kubrick, 1968
Keir Dullea

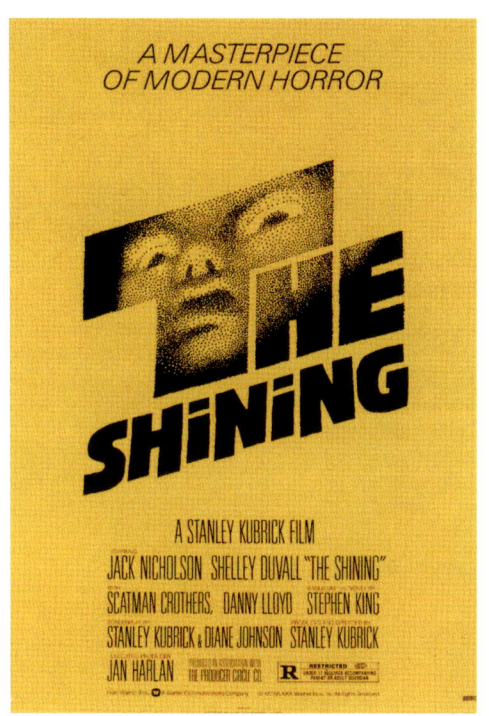

The Shining

Shining
Stanley Kubrick, 1980
Jack Nicholson

Gus Van Sant (1952)
Jennifer Lopez (1969)

"I'm really going in a weird I-don't-know-where direction. I prefer it to anything like what standardized filmmaking has become."

Gus Van Sant

My Own Private Idaho

My Private Idaho
Gus Van Sant, 1991
River Phoenix

T-Men

Geheimagent T / La Brigade du suicide
Anthony Mann, 1947
Dennis O'Keefe, Alfred Ryder

Louise Fletcher (1934)
Paul Schrader (1946)
Willem Dafoe (1955)

Platoon

Oliver Stone, 1986

"What I'm out for is a good time; all the rest is propaganda!"

Arthur Seaton (Albert Finney)

**Saturday Night
and Sunday Morning**

*Samstagnacht bis Sonntagmorgen /
Samedi soir, dimanche matin*
Karel Reisz, 1960
Albert Finney, Shirley Anne Field

Love with the Proper Stranger

Verliebt in einen Fremden /
Une certaine rencontre
Robert Mulligan, 1963
Natalie Wood, Steve McQueen

JULY 19

Atom Egoyan (1960)

Burn After Reading

Ethan Coen, Joel Coen, 2008
George Clooney, Tilda Swinton

"In space no one can
hear you scream."

Alien

Ridley Scott, 1979

James Cagney (1899)
Marcel Dalio (1900)
Donald Sutherland (1935)
Wong Kar-wai (1958)

Grand Illusion

Die große Illusion / La Grande Illusion
Jean Renoir, 1937
Jean Gabin, Marcel Dalio

Ginger Rogers (1911)
Will Ferrell (1967)
Apichatpong Weerasethakul (1970)

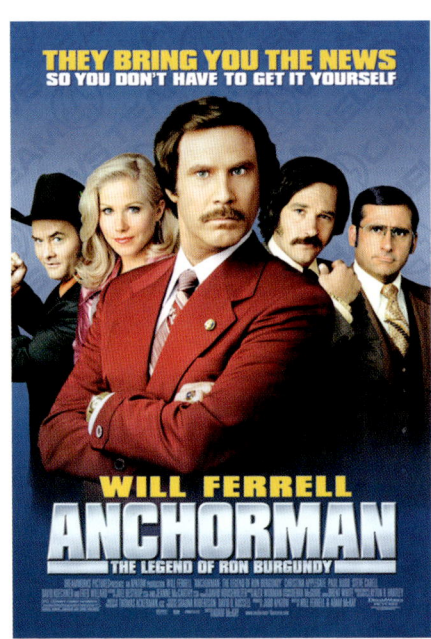

Anchorman:
The Legend of Ron Burgundy

Anchorman – Die Legende von Ron Burgundy / Présentateur vedette : La Légende de Ron Burgundy
Adam McKay, 2004
Will Ferrell

Harry Dean Stanton (1926)
Forest Whitaker (1961)
Diane Kruger (1976)

"I think your death will be the first real thing that has happened to you."

Idi Amin (Forest Whitaker)

The Last King of Scotland

Der letzte König von Schottland – In den Fängen der Macht / Le dernier roi d'Écosse
Kevin Macdonald, 2006
James McAvoy, Forest Whitaker

Ingmar Bergman (1918)
Scott Rudin (1958)

Fanny and Alexander

Fanny und Alexander / Fanny et Alexandre
Ingmar Bergman, 1982
Bertil Guve, Pernilla Allwin

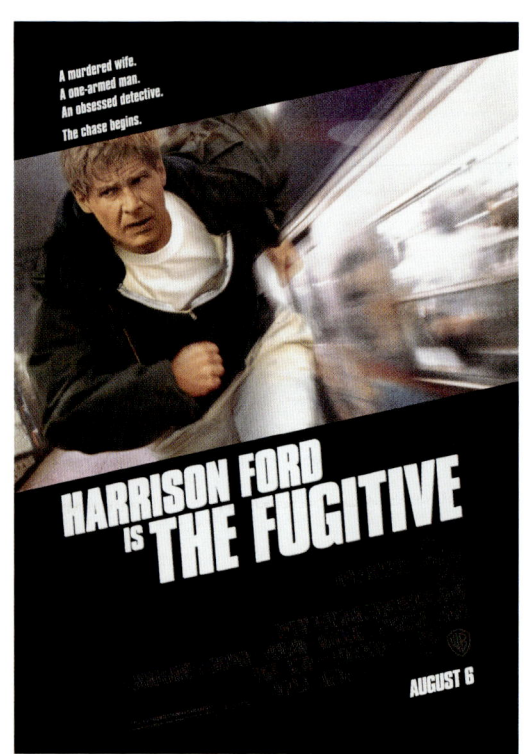

The Fugitive

Auf der Flucht / Le Fugitif
Andrew Davis, 1993
Harrison Ford

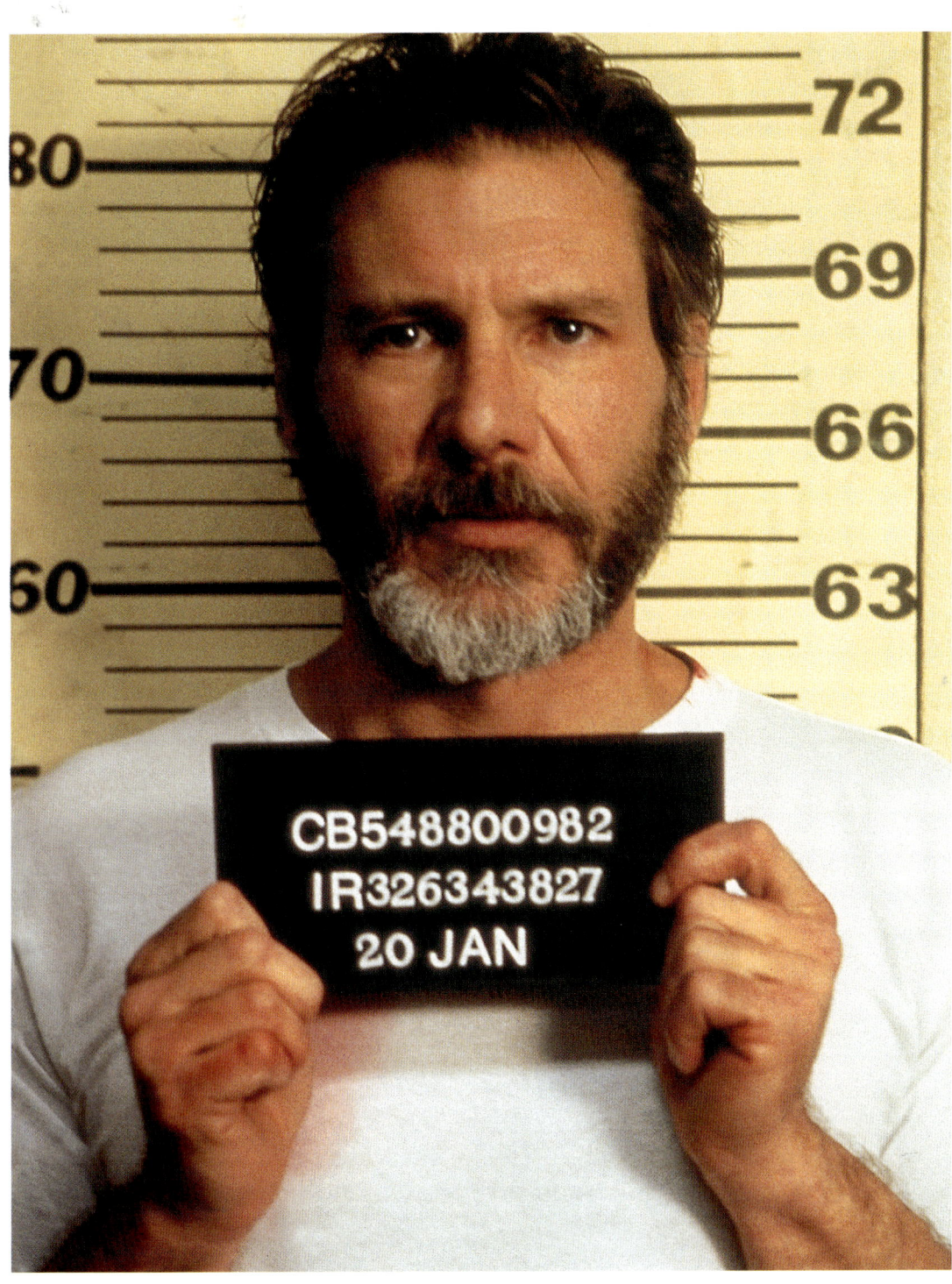

"Truly the most beautiful Technicolor film ever made."

Martin Scorsese

The Red Shoes

Die roten Schuhe / Les Chaussons rouges
Michael Powell, Emeric Pressburger, 1948
Léonide Massine

Fireworks

Hanabi – Feuerblume /
Hana-bi, feux d'artifices
Takeshi Kitano, 1997
Takeshi Kitano

Tura Satana (1938)
Cary Fukunaga (1977)

"Beyond a doubt, the best movie ever made. It is possibly better than any film that will be made in the future."

John Waters

Faster, Pussycat! Kill! Kill!

Die Satansweiber von Tittfield
Russ Meyer, 1965
Tura Satana

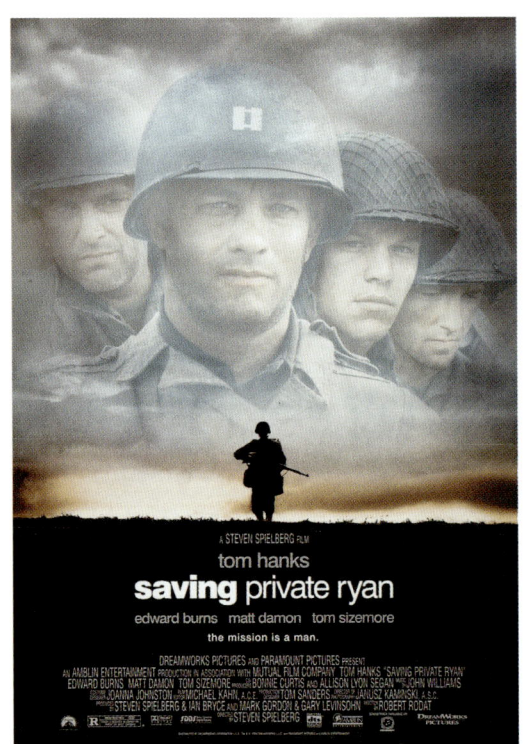

Saving Private Ryan

Der Soldat James Ryan / Il faut sauver le soldat Ryan
Steven Spielberg, 1998
Tom Hanks

"It's like *The Godfather* acted out by the Munsters ... a baroque comedy about people who behave in ordinary ways in grotesque circumstances, and it has the juice of everyday family craziness in it."

Pauline Kael

Prizzi's Honor

Die Ehre der Prizzis / L'Honneur des Prizzi
John Huston, 1985
Anjelica Huston

George Cukor (1899)
Vittorio De Sica (1901)
Bérénice Bejo (1976)

Bicycle Thieves

Fahrraddiebe / Le Voleur de bicyclette
Vittorio De Sica, 1948
Enzo Staiola, Lamberto Maggiorani

"I think the thing that appealed to me was the suddenness of the murder in the shower, coming, as it were, out of the blue. That was about all."

Alfred Hitchcock

On the set of
Psycho

Psychose
Alfred Hitchcock, 1960
Alfred Hitchcock, Janet Leigh

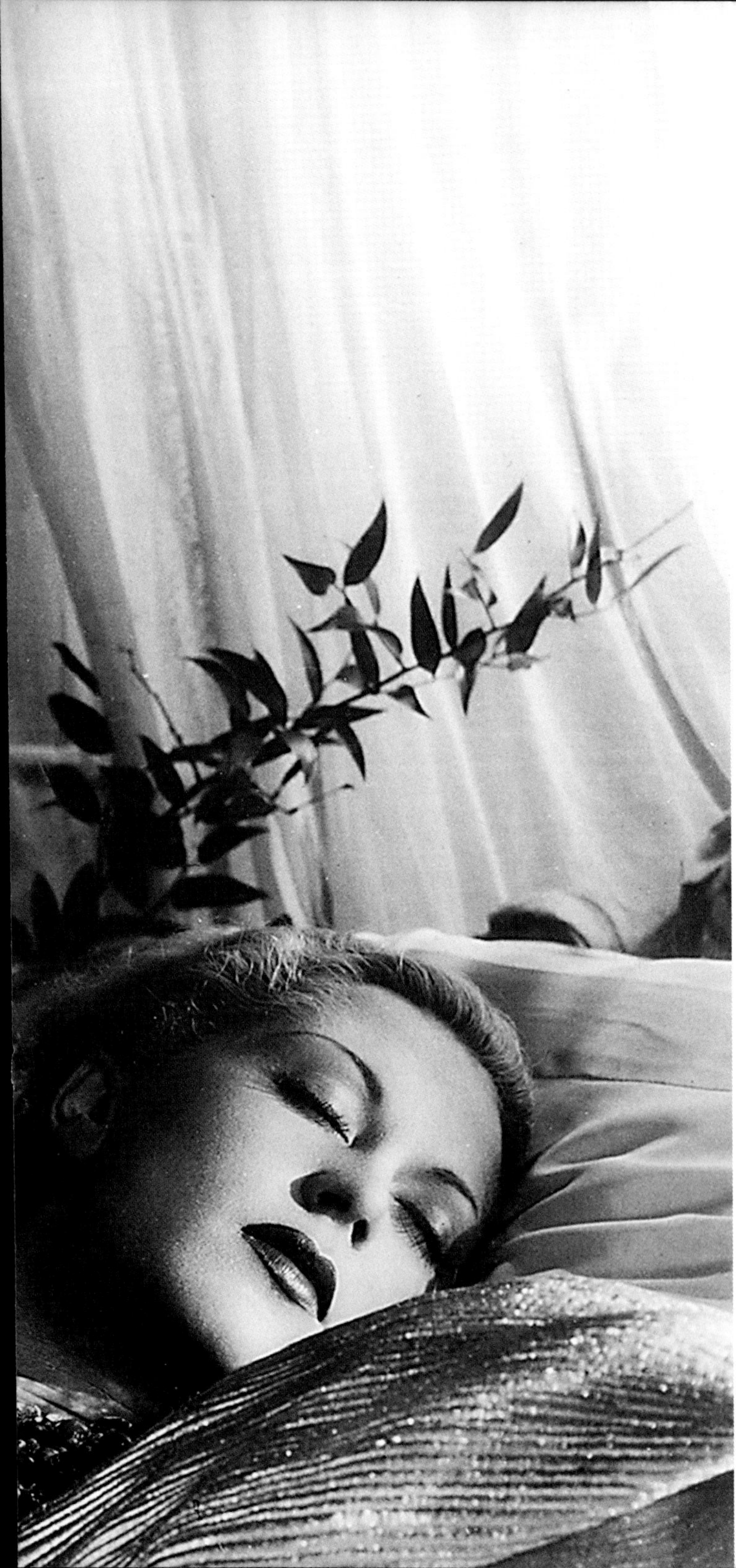

JULY 5

Jean Cocteau (1889)
Eva Green (1980)

Beauty and the Beast

Es war einmal / La Belle et la Bête
Jean Cocteau, 1946
Jean Marais, Josette Day

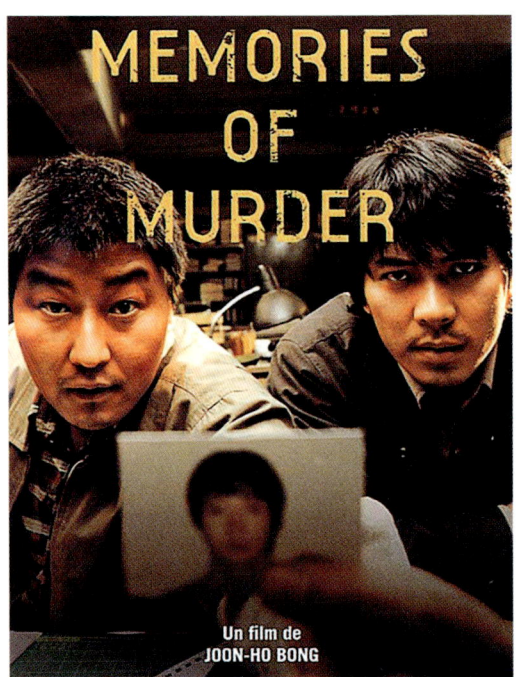

Memories of Murder

Joon-ho Bong, 2003
Kang-ho Song, Sang-kyung Kim

George Sanders (1906)
Tom Stoppard (1937)
Tom Cruise (1962)

A Few Good Men

Eine Frage der Ehre / Des hommes d'honneur
Rob Reiner, 1992
Tom Cruise

"John Malkovich is the ideal actor to play, well, John Malkovich."

New York Magazine

Being John Malkovich

Dans la peau de John Malkovich
Spike Jonze, 1999
John Malkovich

Charles Laughton (1899)
William Wyler (1902)
Olivia de Havilland (1916)
Sydney Pollack (1934)

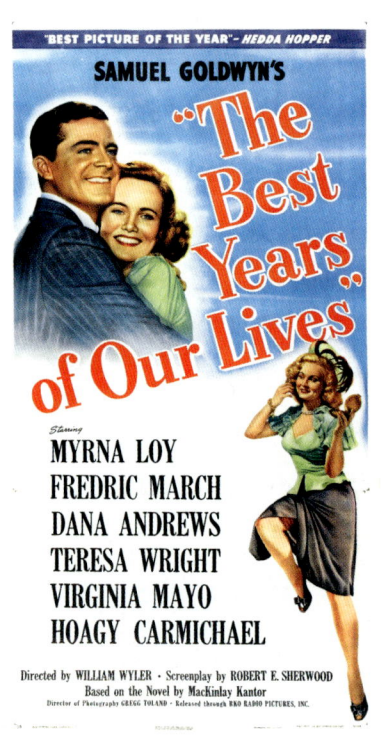

The Best Years of Our Lives

Die besten Jahre unseres Lebens /
Les Plus Belles Années de notre vie
William Wyler, 1946
Myrna Loy, Fredric March

*"**Mother + Father** is a technological tour de force, every bit as slickly edited as the original Hollywood movies so ingeniously cannibalised in the course of its making."*

The Sunday Telegraph

Mother + Father

Candice Breitz, 2005
Diane Keaton, Faye Dunaway,
Shirley MacLaine, Meryl Streep,
Susan Sarandon, Julia Roberts

Bernard Herrmann (1911)
Robert Evans (1930)

"His sword made him a hero...
his courage made him a legend.
This summer, justice is blind."

Zatoichi

Zatoichi – Der blinde Samurai
Takeshi Kitano, 2003
Takeshi Kitano

Mel Brooks (1926)
John Cusack (1966)

"It takes two to love, as it takes two to hate.
And I will keep loving you, in spite of yourself.
My heart beats faster when I think of you.
Nothing else matters."

Marion Steiner (Catherine Deneuve)

The Last Metro

Die letzte Metro / Le Dernier Métro
François Truffaut, 1980
Catherine Deneuve, Heinz Bennent

Krzysztof Kieslowski (1941)
Isabelle Adjani (1955)
Janusz Kaminski (1959)

Three Colors: Blue

Drei Farben: Blau / Trois couleurs : Bleu
Krzysztof Kieslowski, 1993
Juliette Binoche

Peter Lorre (1904)
Paul Thomas Anderson (1970)

M

M – Eine Stadt sucht einen Mörder / M le maudit
Fritz Lang, 1931
Peter Lorre

"War is an extreme situation which can change the nature of man. For this reason, I consider it to be the greatest sin."

Kon Ichikawa

The Burmese Harp

Die Harfe von Burma / La Harpe de Birmanie
Kon Ichikawa, 1956
Shôji Yasui

Georgia Hale (1905)
Claude Chabrol (1930)

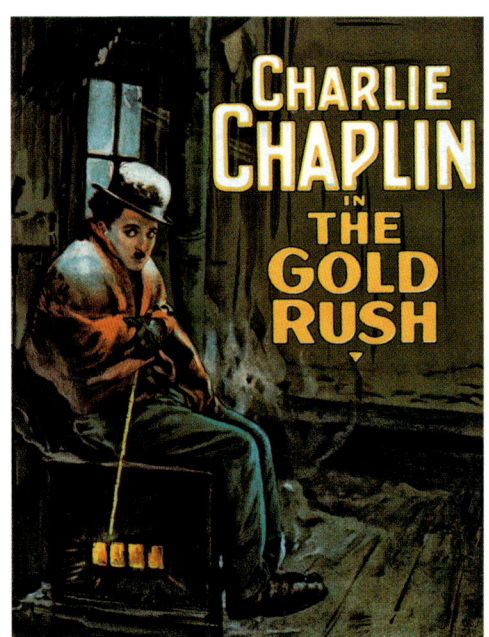

The Gold Rush

Goldrausch / La Ruée vers l'or
Charlie Chaplin, 1925
Charlie Chaplin

Little Miss Sunshine

Jonathan Dayton and Valerie Faris, 2005
Abigail Breslin

Billy Wilder (1906)
Kris Kristofferson (1936)
Meryl Streep (1949)
Stephen Chow (1962)

The African Queen

L'Odyssée de l'African Queen
John Huston, 1951
Humphrey Bogart, Katharine Hepburn

Jane Russell (1921)
Lalo Schifrin (1932)

"*Days of Heaven* is above all one of the most beautiful films ever made."

Roger Ebert

Days of Heaven

In der Glut des Südens / Les Moissons du ciel
Terrence Malick, 1978
Richard Gere

Dogville

Lars von Trier, 2003
Nicole Kidman

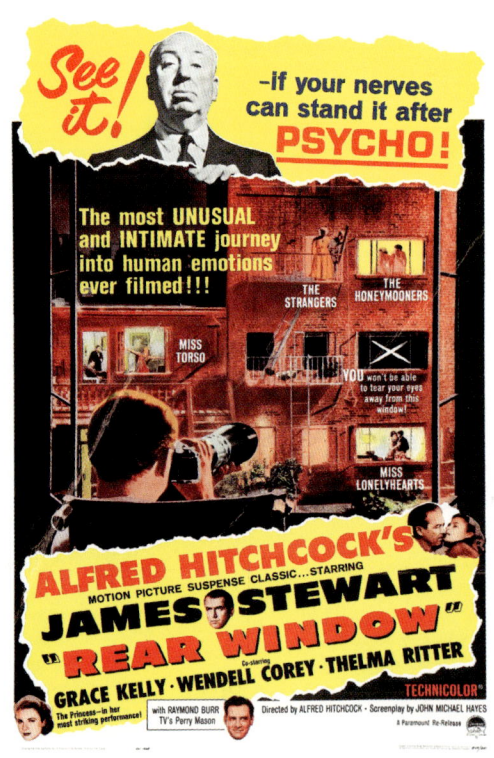

Rear Window

Das Fenster zum Hof / Fenêtre sur cour
Alfred Hitchcock, 1954
James Stewart, Grace Kelly

Isabella Rossellini (1952)

Blue Velvet

David Lynch, 1986
Dennis Hopper, Isabella Rossellini

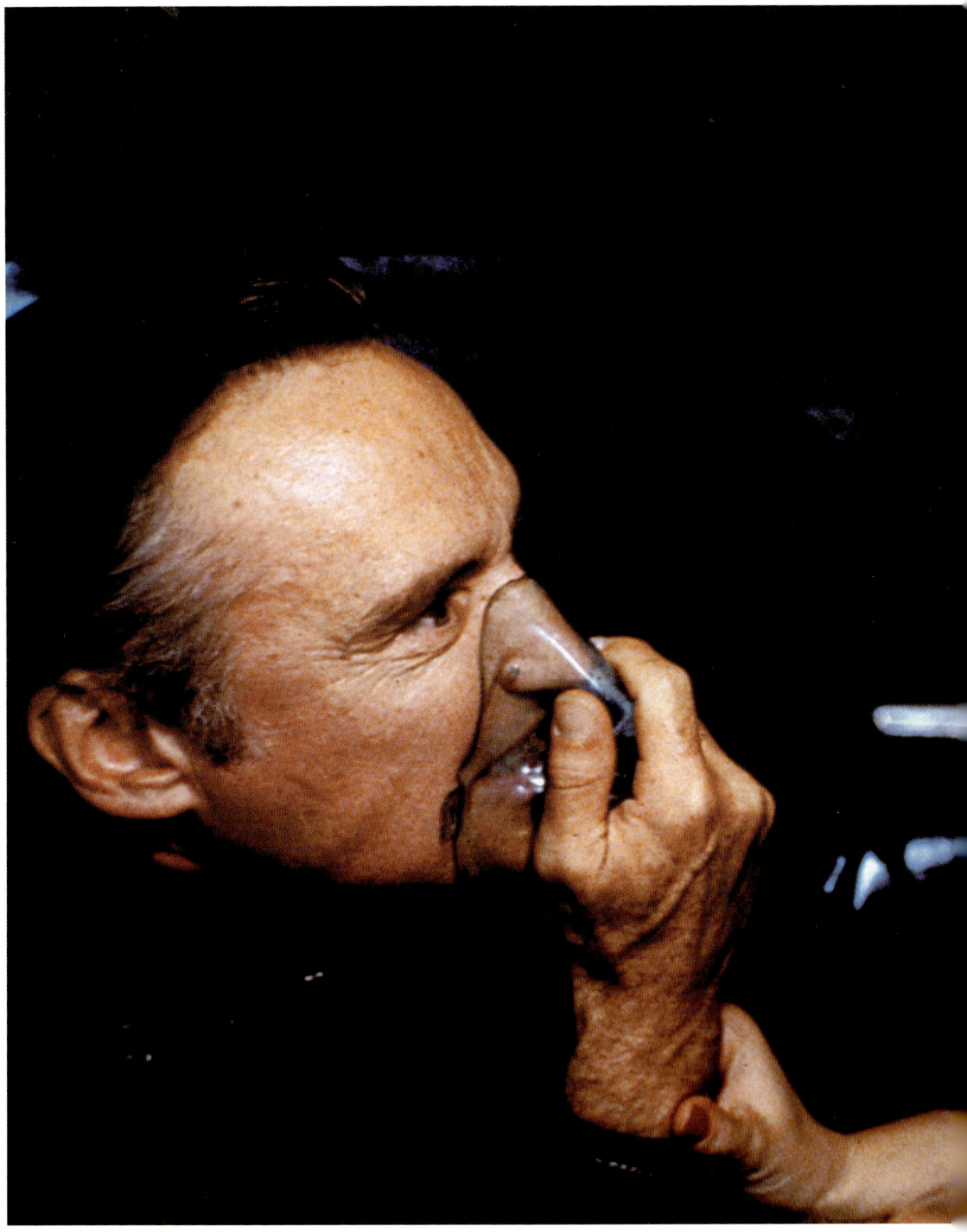

"Serve the public trust. Protect the innocent. Uphold the law."

Officer Alex J. Murphy / RoboCop (Peter Weller)

RoboCop

Paul Verhoeven, 1987
Peter Weller

–"You remember how dumb I used to be?"
–"Yeah?"
–"Well, I'm better now."

Stan (Stan Laurel) and Ollie (Oliver Hardy)

Block-Heads

Die Klotzköpfe / Têtes de pioche
John G. Blystone, 1938
Oliver Hardy, Stan Laurel

JUNE 15

Helen Hunt (1963)

As Good as It Gets

Besser geht's nicht /
Pour le pire et pour le meilleur
James L. Brooks, 1997
Helen Hunt, Jack Nicholson

Dance of the Vampires

Tanz der Vampire / Le Bal des vampires
Roman Polanski, 1966
Roman Polanski, Sharon Tate

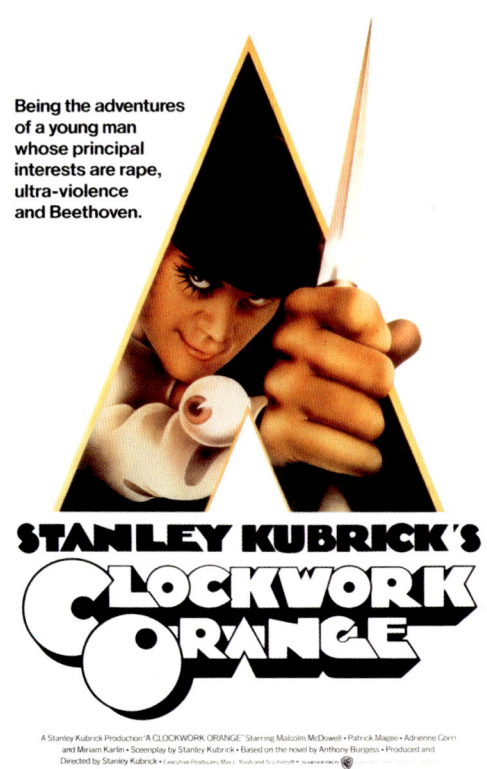

Being the adventures of a young man whose principal interests are rape, ultra-violence and Beethoven.

A Clockwork Orange

Uhrwerk Orange / Orange mécanique
Stanley Kubrick, 1971
Malcolm McDowell

"In its lived-in, completely non-ideological way, *Winter's Bone* is one of the great feminist works in film."

The New Yorker

Winter's Bone

Debra Granik, 2009
Jennifer Lawrence

The Spy Who Came in from the Cold

Der Spion, der aus der Kälte kam /
L'espion qui venait du froid
Martin Ritt, 1965
Richard Burton

Judy Garland (1922)

"Whereas you need nostalgia to get through *White Christmas*, you can be the vilest cynic and still like Minnelli's fluent four-act examination of a nice middle-class St. Louis family and its ups and downs circa 1903."

The Observer

Meet Me in St. Louis

Le Chant du Missouri
Vincente Minelli, 1944
Judy Garland

Johnny Depp (1963)
Natalie Portman (1981)

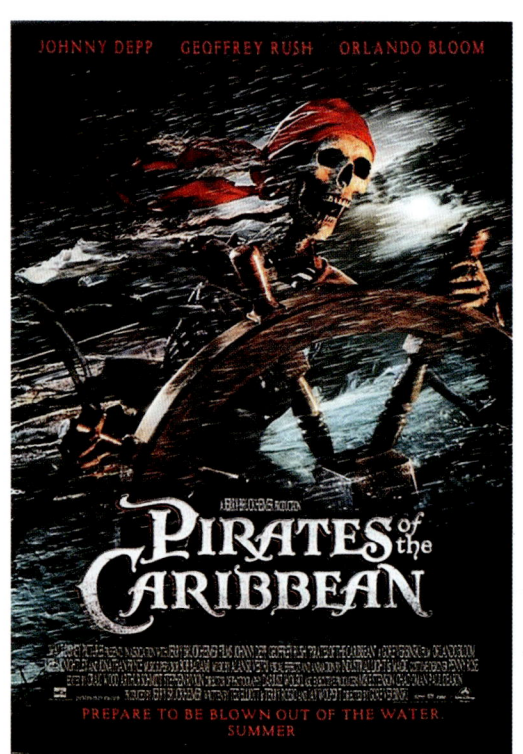

Pirates of the Caribbean:
The Curse of the Black Pearl

Fluch der Karibik / Pirates des Caraïbes :
La Malédiction du Black Pearl
Gore Verbinski, 2003
Keira Knightley, Johnny Depp

"You only live once …
so see *The Pink Panther* twice!!!"

The Pink Panther

Der rosarote Panther / La Panthère rose
Blake Edwards, 1964
Capucine, David Niven

Jessica Tandy (1909)
Dean Martin (1917)

Rocky

John G. Avildsen, 1976
Sylvester Stallone

Aaron Sorkin (1961)
Paul Giamatti (1967)

Sideways

Alexander Payne, 2004
Thomas Haden Church, Paul Giamatti

To Have and Have Not

Haben und Nichthaben / Le Port de l'angoisse
Howard Hawks, 1944
Hoagy Carmichael, Lauren Bacall

Angelina Jolie (1975)

"Insanity runs in my family ... It practically gallops."

Mortimer Brewster (Cary Grant)

Arsenic and Old Lace

Arsen und Spitzenhäubchen /
Arsenic et vieilles dentelles
Frank Capra, 1942/44
Peter Lorre

–"You're NOT a girl! You're a GUY! Why would a guy wanna marry a guy?" –"Security!"

Joe (Tony Curtis) and Jerry (Jack Lemmon)

Some Like It Hot

Manche mögen's heiß / Certains l'aiment chaud
Billy Wilder, 1959
Tony Curtis, Jack Lemmon, Marilyn Monroe

Johnny Weissmuller (1904)

−"Jane. Tarzan. Jane.
Tarzan. Jane. Tarzan. Jane.
Tarzan. Jane. Tarzan. Jane ... "
−"Oh, please stop!"

Tarzan (Johnny Weissmuller) and
Jane (Maureen O'Sullivan)

Tarzan the Ape Man

Tarzan, der Affenmensch / Tarzan, l'homme singe
W. S. Van Dyke, 1932
Johnny Weissmuller, Maureen O'Sullivan

Marilyn Monroe (1926)
Morgan Freeman (1937)

The funny, touching and totally irresistible story
of a working relationship that became a
25-year friendship.

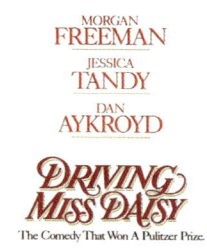

Driving Miss Daisy

Miss Daisy und ihr Chauffeur /
Miss Daisy et son chauffeur
Bruce Beresford, 1989
Morgan Freeman

Clint Eastwood (1930)
Rainer Werner Fassbinder (1945)
Colin Farrell (1976)

The Bridges of Madison County

Die Brücken am Fluss / Sur la route de Madison
Clint Eastwood, 1995

"I'm paid to risk my neck. I'll decide where and when I'll do it. This isn't it."

Cole (John Wayne)

El Dorado

Howard Hawks, 1966
Michele Carey, James Caan

Due Date

Stichtag – Schluss mit gemütlich /
Date Limite
Todd Phillips, 2010
Zach Galifianakis, Robert Downey Jr.

"A wry psychological comedy about a man who prefers his cat to his two wives. The tart flavor of the film derives from the familial nastiness: one can't like any of them, one can't even really like the cat."

Pauline Kael

A Cat, Two Women, and One Man

Shirô Toyoda, 1956
Hisaya Morishige

MAY 27

Vincent Price (1911)
Christopher Lee (1922)

Edward Scissorhands

Edward mit den Scherenhänden /
Edward aux mains d'argent
Tim Burton, 1990
Johnny Depp

Paul Lukas (1891)
John Wayne (1907)
Helena Bonham Carter (1966)

"This is, no doubt about it, a tour de force, a work that fully lives up to its director's ambitions. It takes a long time to purge Tchaikovsky from your head: You exit, pursued by a swan."

New York Magazine

Black Swan

Darren Aronofsky, 2010
Natalie Portman

Ian McKellen (1939)
Frank Oz (1944)
Mike Myers (1963)
Cillian Murphy (1976)

The Lord of the Rings:
The Return of the King

*Der Herr der Ringe: Die Rückkehr des
Königs / Le Seigneur des anneaux: Le
Retour du roi*
Peter Jackson, 2003
Ian McKellen

"An exercise in urban paranoia and mental disintegration that echoes or anticipates everything from *Repulsion* and *Rosemary's Baby* to *Bitter Moon* and *The Pianist*."

The Village Voice

The Tenant

Der Mieter / Le Locataire
Roman Polanski, 1976
Roman Polanski

On the set of
A Foreign Affair

Eine auswärtige Affäre /
La Scandaleuse de Berlin
Billy Wilder, 1948
Hedy Lamarr, Billy Wilder,
Marlene Dietrich

Laurence Olivier (1907)
Charles Aznavour (1924)

Shoot the Piano Player

Schießen Sie auf den Pianisten /
Tirez sur le pianiste
François Truffaut, 1960
Marie Dubois, Charles Aznavour

On the set of
The Birds

Die Vögel / Les Oiseaux
Alfred Hitchcock, 1963

James Stewart (1908)
Cher (1946)

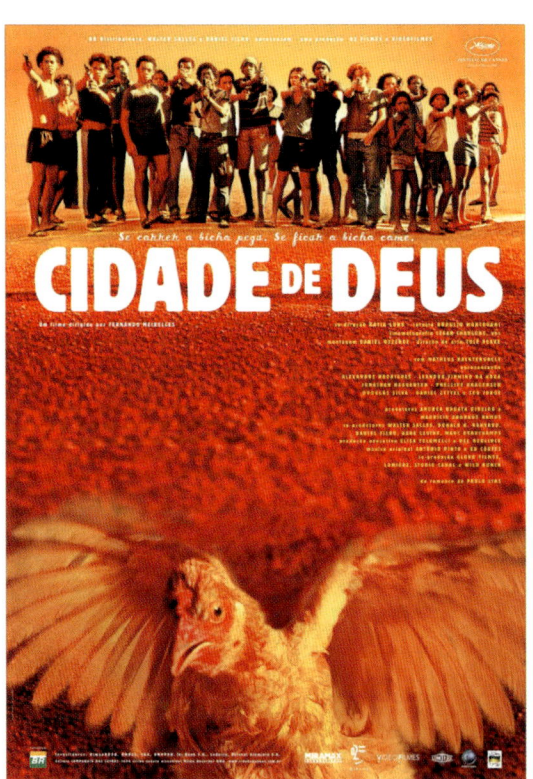

City of God

La Cité de Dieu
Fernando Meirelles, 2002
Alexandre Rodrigues

"God gave me the talent to pose
for pictures and it seems to
make people happy. That can't
be a bad thing, can it?"

Bettie Page (Gretchen Mol)

The Notorious Bettie Page

Mary Harron, 2005
Gretchen Mol

Frank Capra (1897)

—"Your ego is absolutely colossal."
—"Yeah, yeah, not bad, how's yours?"

Ellie (Claudette Colbert) to Peter (Clark Gable)

It Happened One Night

Es geschah in einer Nacht / New York–Miami
Frank Capra, 1934
Clark Gable, Claudette Colbert

Jean Gabin (1904)
Dennis Hopper (1936)

"Gabin could express the most violent emotion with a mere quiver of his impassive face."

Jean Renoir

La Bête humaine

Bestie Mensch
Jean Renoir, 1938
Jean Gabin

Henry Fonda (1905)
Pierce Brosnan (1953)
Debra Winger (1955)

"Because neither Kit nor Port had ever lived a life of regularity, they had made the fatal error of coming to regard time as nonexistent. One year was like another. Eventually everything would happen."

Paul Bowles

The Sheltering Sky

Himmel über der Wüste / Un thé au Sahara
Bernardo Bertolucci, 1990
Debra Winger

"Since producer James B. Harris and director Stanley Kubrick are men of talent, there is much about the film that is excellent. James Mason has never been better than he is as the erudite Humbert Humbert, driven by a furious passion for a rather slovenly, perverse 'nymphet.'"

Variety

Lolita

Stanley Kubrick, 1962
James Mason, Sue Lyon

George Lucas (1944)
Robert Zemeckis (1951)
Cate Blanchett (1969)
Sofia Coppola (1971)

Star Wars Episode IV: A New Hope

Krieg der Sterne / Star Wars, épisode IV:
Un nouvel espoir
George Lucas, 1977
C-3PO, R2-D2

Bathing Beauty

Badende Venus / Le Bal des sirènes
George Sidney, 1944
Red Skelton

Katharine Hepburn (1907)
Barry Ackroyd (1954)

"Hurrah for that little difference."

Adam Bonner (Spencer Tracy) to Amanda Bonner (Katharine Hepburn)

Adam's Rib

Ehekrieg / Madame porte la culotte
George Cukor, 1949
Spencer Tracy, Katharine Hepburn

The Blue Angel

Der blaue Engel / L'Ange bleu
Josef von Sternberg, 1930
Marlene Dietrich

"In Italy for 30 years under the Borgias they had warfare, terror, murder, and bloodshed, but they produced Michelangelo, Leonardo da Vinci, and the Renaissance. In Switzerland they had brotherly love — they had 500 years of democracy and peace, and what did that produce? The cuckoo clock. So long, Holly."

Harry Lime (Orson Welles)

The Third Man

Der dritte Mann / Le Troisième Homme
Carol Reed, 1949
Bernard Lee, Joseph Cotten,
Trevor Howard

Glenda Jackson (1936)
Rosario Dawson (1979)

"Your favorite fire-breathing monster ... Like you've never seen him before!"

The Return of Godzilla

Godzilla – Die Rückkehr des Monsters /
Le Retour de Godzilla
Koji Hashimoto, 1984
Godzilla

Fernandel (1903)

"Your hands were made for blessing, not for striking."

God to Don Camillo (Fernandel)

The Little World of Don Camillo

Don Camillo und Peppone /
Le Petit Monde de Don Camillo
Julien Duvivier, 1952
Fernandel

Gary Cooper (1901)
Anne Baxter (1923)

High Noon

Zwölf Uhr mittags / Le Train sifflera trois fois
Fred Zinnemann, 1952
Gary Cooper

MAY 6

Rudolph Valentino (1895)
Max Ophüls (1902)
Orson Welles (1915)
George Clooney (1961)

"It comes close to being the most sensational film ever made in Hollywood."

The New York Times

Citizen Kane

Orson Welles, 1941
Orson Welles

Tyrone Power (1914)
Michael Palin (1943)
Richard E. Grant (1957)

A Fish Called Wanda

Ein Fisch namens Wanda /
Un poisson nommé Wanda
Charles Crichton, 1987
Michael Palin

Breakfast at Tiffany's

Frühstück bei Tiffany / Diamants sur canapé
Blake Edwards, 1961
George Peppard, Audrey Hepburn

Bing Crosby (1902)
Mary Astor (1906)

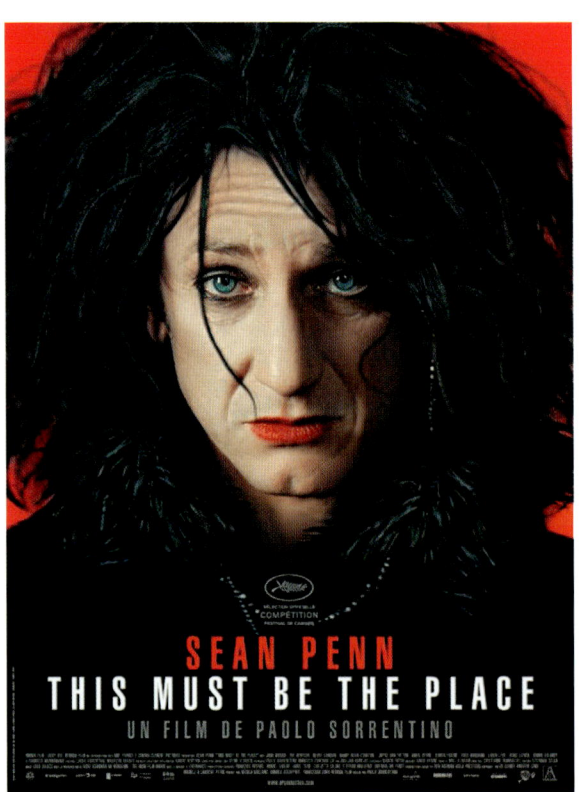

Cheyenne – This Must Be the Place

Paolo Sorrentino, 2011
Sean Penn

Chungking Express

Wong Kar-wai, 1994
Faye Wong

"Let's never come here again, because it would never be as much fun."

Charlotte (Scarlett Johansson) to Bob (Bill Murray)

Lost in Translation

Sofia Coppola, 2003
Bill Murray, Scarlett Johansson

Jacques Audiard (1952)
Jane Campion (1954)
Lars von Trier (1956)
Kirsten Dunst (1982)

Heaven Can Wait

Ein himmlischer Sünder / Le ciel peut attendre
Ernst Lubitsch, 1943
Don Ameche, Gene Tierney

Fred Zinneman (1907)
Michelle Pfeiffer (1958)
Uma Thurman (1970)

Gattaca

Bienvenue à Gattaca
Andrew Niccol, 1997
Uma Thurman

Ann-Margret (1941)
Mary McDonnell (1952)
Penélope Cruz (1974)
Jessica Alba (1981)

"You're still searching for me in every woman."

Maria Elena (Penélope Cruz)

Vicky Cristina Barcelona

Woody Allen, 2008
Penélope Cruz

"I used to cry when I watched Chaplin's films. It was from him that I learned the role of the underdog. Because I'm also from a poor family, this kind of thing moved me."

Stephen Chow

Kung Fu Hustle

Crazy Kung-Fu
Stephen Chow, 2004
Stephen Chow

"Not widely seen, *Victor and Victoria* (1933) is now known, if known at all, as the source of Blake Edwards' remake, *Victor/Victoria* (1982) ... On its own merits, *Victor and Victoria* stands as a remarkable example of late Weimar popular cinema and easily takes its place alongside contemporary Hollywood work by Ernst Lubitsch."

senses of cinema

Victor and Victoria

Viktor und Viktoria
Reinhold Schünzel, 1933
Hermann Thimig, Renate Müller

Al Pacino (1940)
Renée Zellweger (1969)

Scarface

Brian De Palma, 1983
Al Pacino

The Young and the Damned

Die Vergessenen / Los Olvidados
Luis Buñuel, 1950
Roberto Cobo

Shirley Temple (1928)
Michael Moore (1954)

"Well, here's my first question: Do you think it's kind of dangerous handing out guns at a bank?"

Michael Moore

Bowling for Columbine

Michael Moore, 2002
Michael Moore

Jack Nicholson (1937)
Johnnie To (1955)

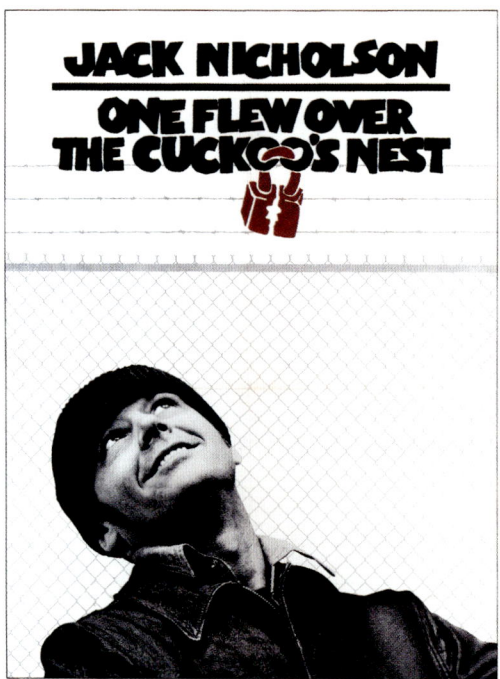

One Flew Over the Cuckoo's Nest

Einer flog über das Kuckucksnest /
Vol au-dessus d'un nid de coucou
Miloš Forman, 1975
Jack Nicholson

Anthony Quinn (1915)
Jean-Pierre Dardenne (1951)

"A man needs a little madness, or else he never dares cut the rope and be free."

Alexis Zorba (Anthony Quinn)

Zorba the Greek

Alexis Sorbas / Zorba le Grec
Michael Cacoyannis, 1964
Alan Bates, Anthony Quinn

Jessica Lange (1949)

"I was a better man with you as a woman than I ever was with a woman as a man..."

Michael Dorsey (Dustin Hoffman)

Tootsie

Sydney Pollack, 1982
Dustin Hoffman

George O'Brien (1899)
Jayne Mansfield (1933)
Kate Hudson (1979)

The Black Swan

Der Seeräuber
Henry King, 1942
Tyrone Power

Miklós Rózsa (1907)
Clive Revill (1930)
David Tennant (1971)

Ben-Hur

William Wyler, 1959
Charlton Heston

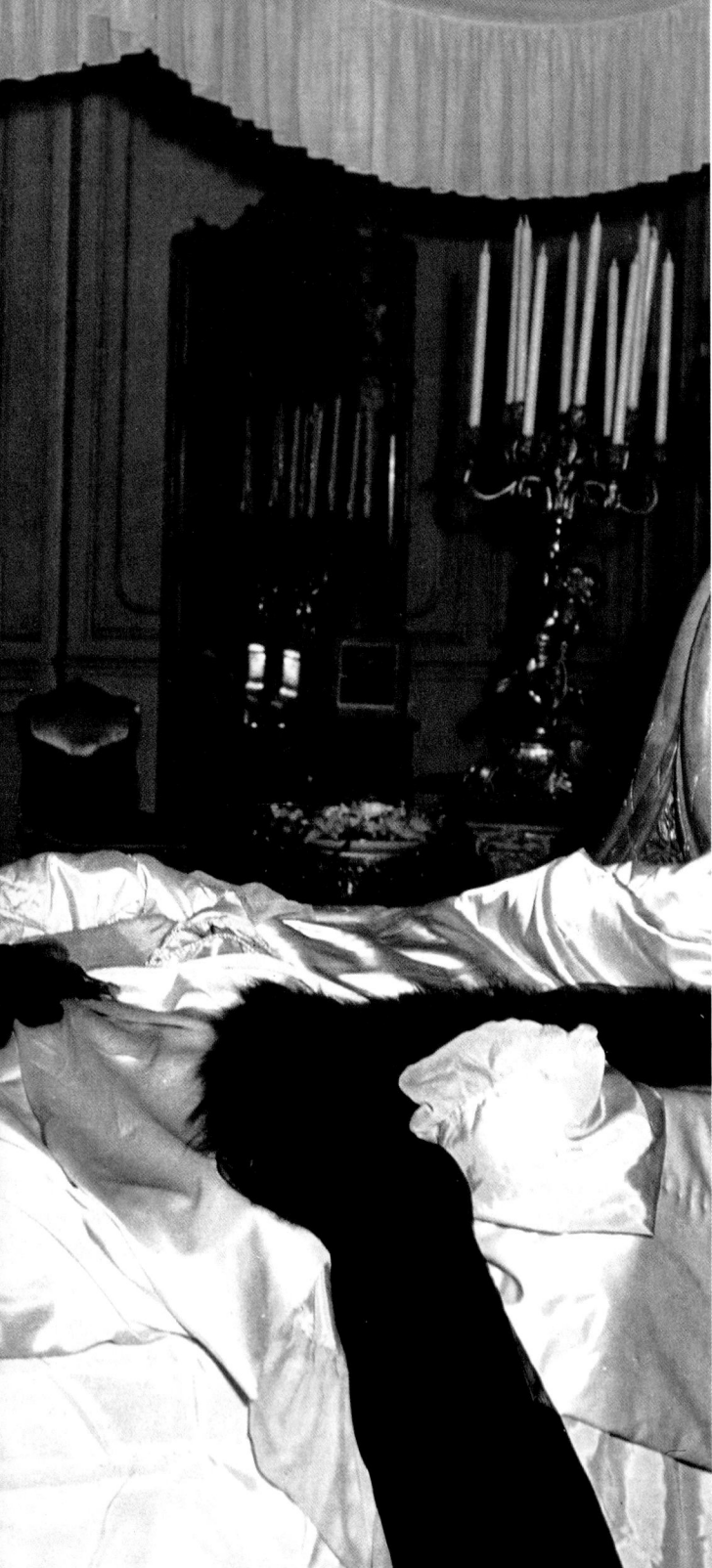

Sunset Boulevard

Boulevard der Dämmerung /
Boulevard du crépuscule
Billy Wilder, 1950
Gloria Swanson, William Holden

Charlie Chaplin (1889)
Peter Ustinov (1921)

"Time is the best author. It always writes the perfect ending."

Calvero (Charlie Chaplin)

Limelight

Rampenlicht / Les Feux de la rampe
Charlie Chaplin, 1952
Claire Bloom, Charlie Chaplin

Claudia Cardinale (1938)
Emma Thompson (1959)
Emma Watson (1990)

"They stole his mind. Now he wants it back. Get ready for the ride of your life."

Total Recall

Total Recall – die totale Erinnerung
Paul Verhoeven, 1990
Arnold Schwarzenegger

The Pianist

Der Pianist / Le Pianiste
Roman Polanski, 2002
Adrien Brody

"Damn! Would you please be a little more careful?"

Hellboy (Ron Perlman)

Hellboy

Guillermo Del Toro, 2004
Rupert Evans, Ron Perlman

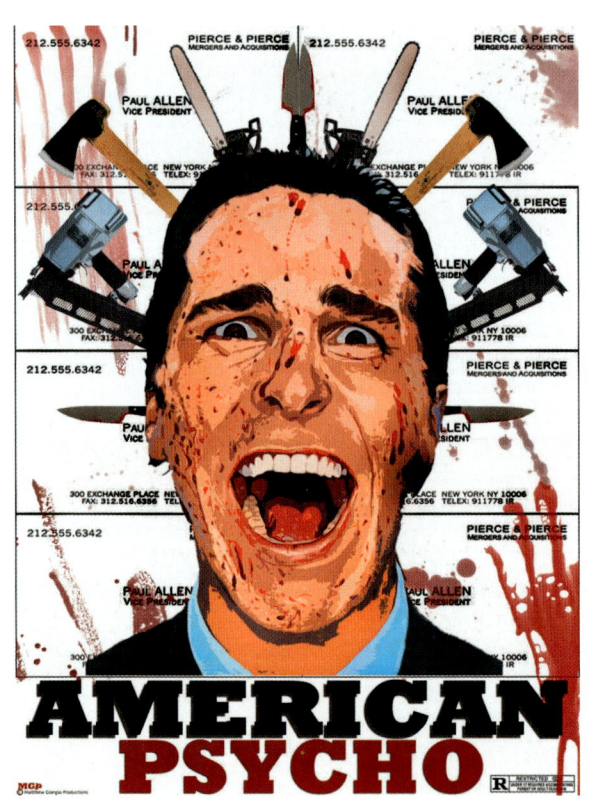

American Psycho

Mary Harron, 2000
Christian Bale

"A pinnacle of the Hollywood fantastic."

Village Voice

The Phantom of the Opera

Das Phantom der Oper / Le Fantôme de l'Opéra
Rupert Julian, 1925
Lon Chaney

Max von Sydow (1929)
Omar Sharif (1932)
Peter Morgan (1963)

Doctor Zhivago

Doktor Schiwago / Le Docteur Jivago
David Lean, 1965
Omar Sharif

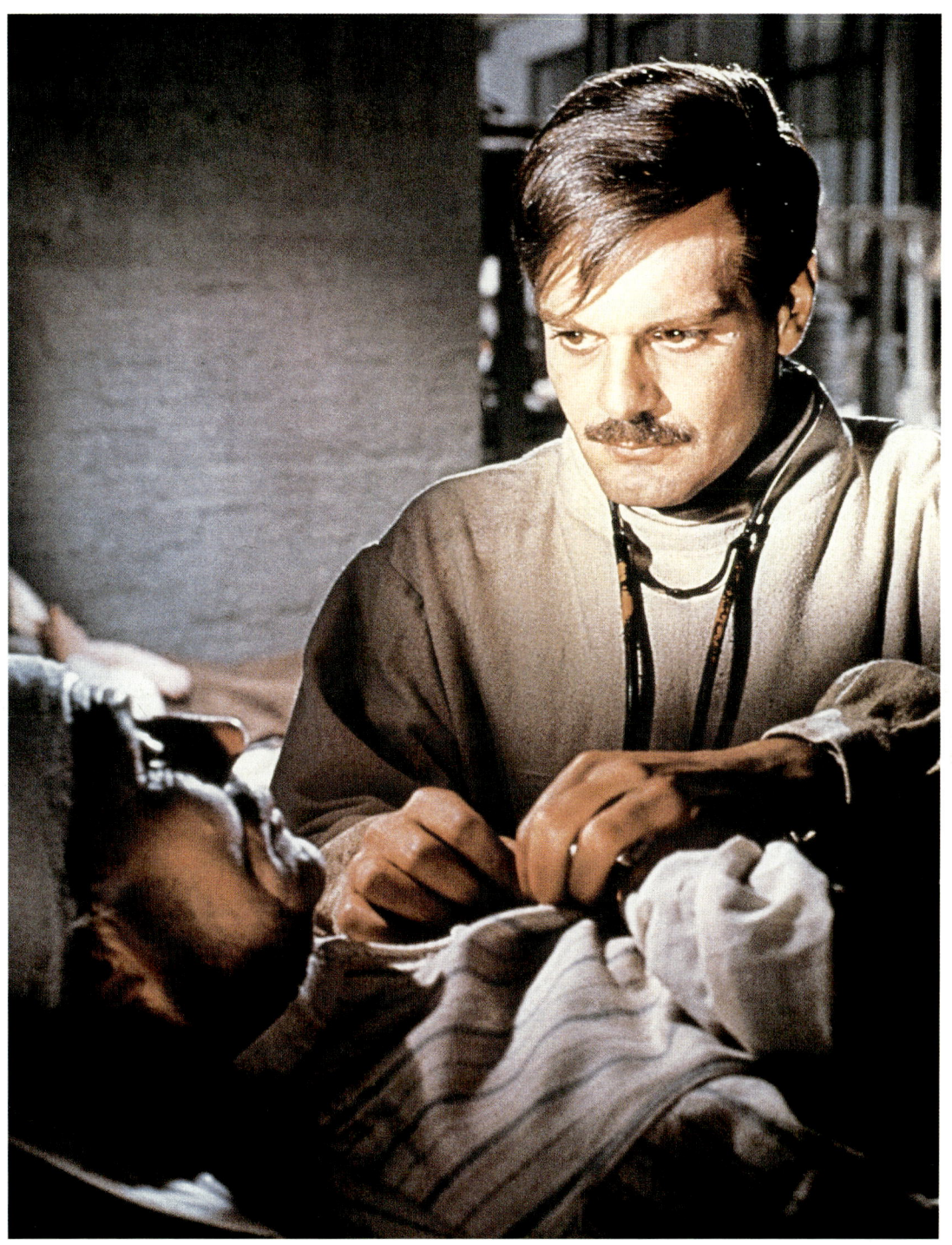

Jean-Paul Belmondo (1933)
Dennis Quaid (1954)

Pierrot le fou

Elf Uhr nachts
Jean-Luc Godard, 1965
Jean-Paul Belmondo

APRIL 8

Mary Pickford (1892)

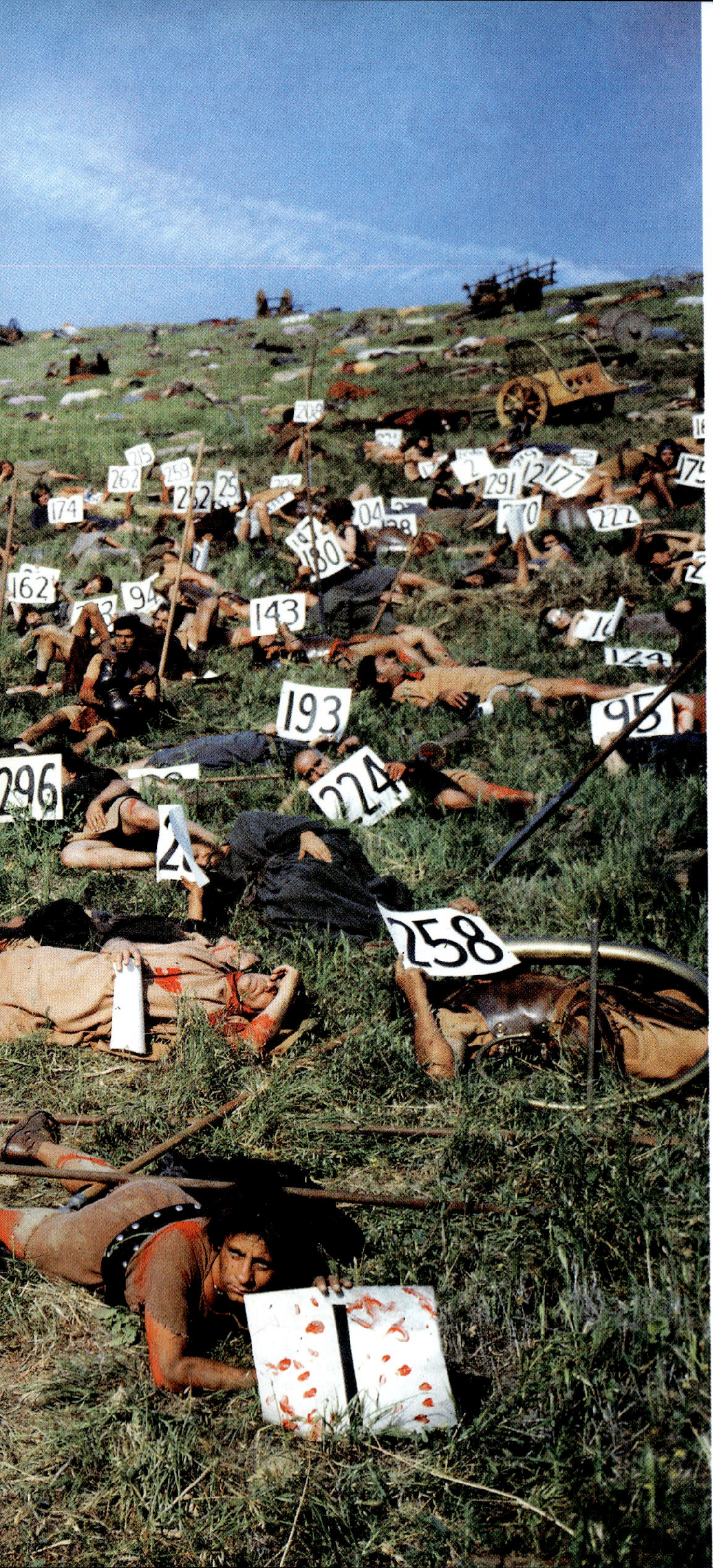

On the set of
Spartacus

Stanley Kubrick, 1960

"No, we haven't met. You've never seen me."

Jane (Vanessa Redgrave)

Blow-Up

Michelangelo Antonioni, 1966
Vanessa Redgrave

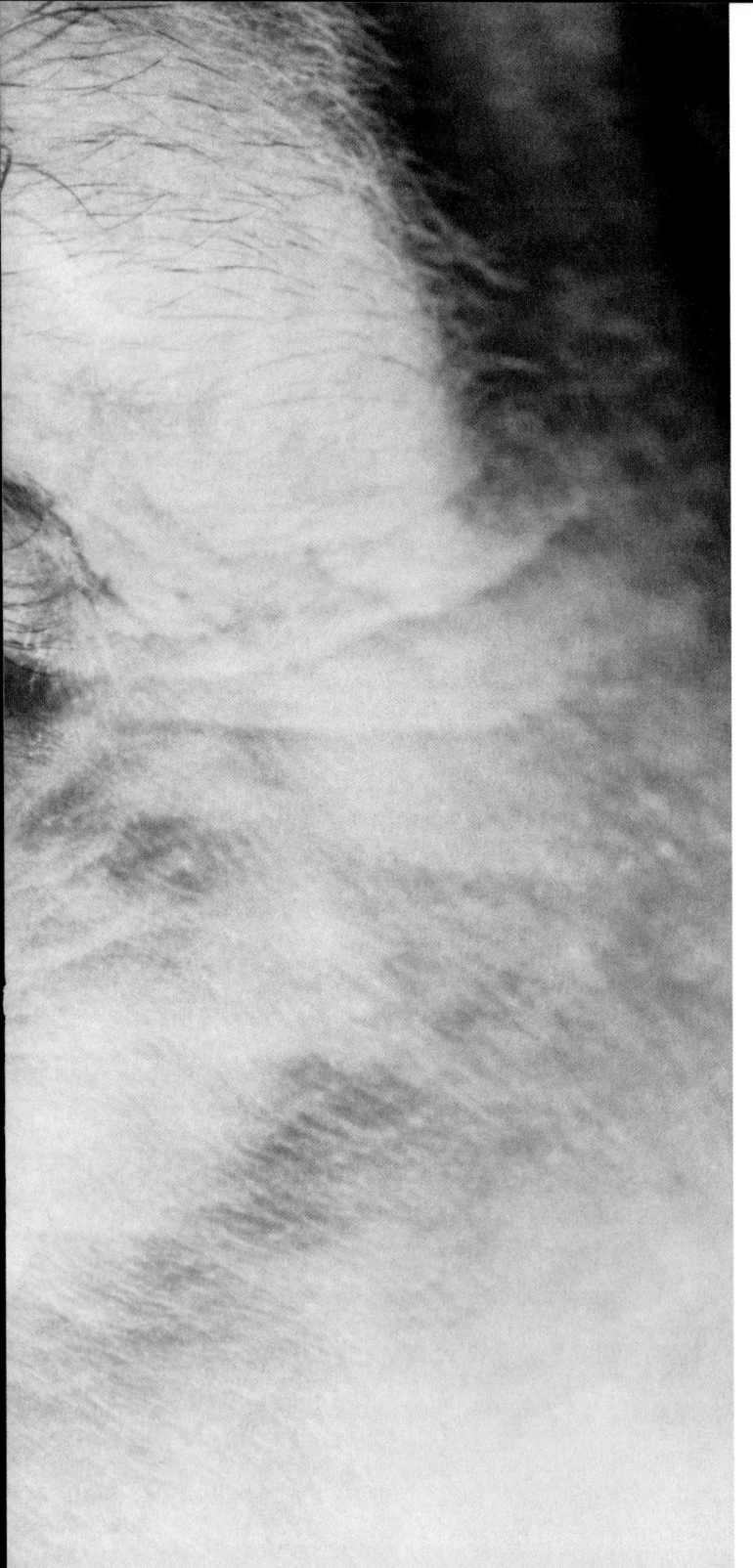

The Spiral Staircase

Die Wendeltreppe / Deux mains, la nuit
Robert Siodmak, 1945
George Brent

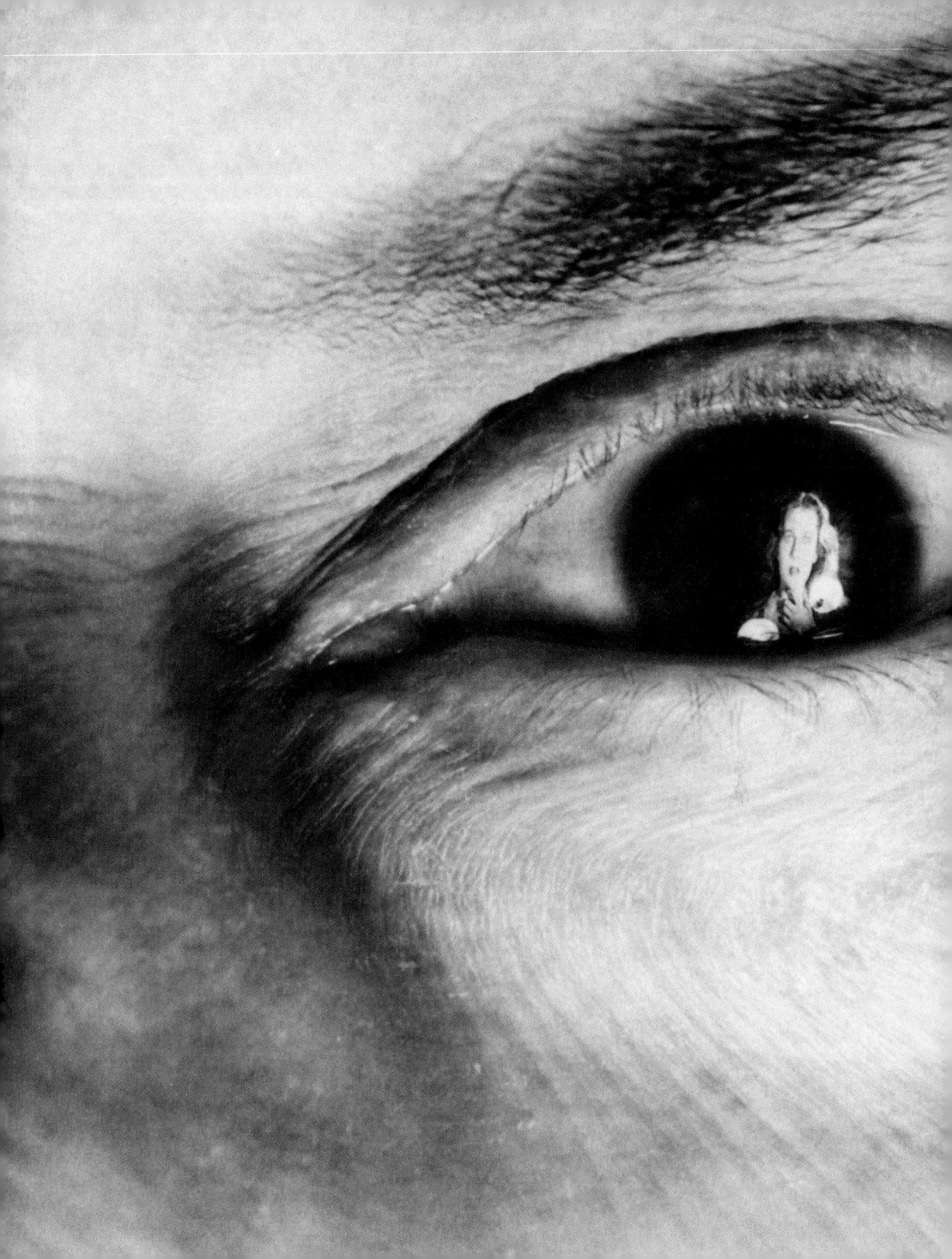

Spencer Tracy (1900)
Bette Davis (1908)
Gregory Peck (1916)
Peter Greenaway (1942)

"Louis, I think this is the beginning of a beautiful friendship."

Rick Blaine (Humphrey Bogart)

Casablanca

Michael Curtiz, 1942
Ingrid Bergman, Humphrey Bogart

Andrei Tarkovsky (1932)
Anthony Perkins (1932)
Robert Downey Jr. (1965)
Heath Ledger (1979)

"Love is a force of nature."

Brokeback Mountain

Le Secret de Brokeback Mountain
Ang Lee, 2005
Heath Ledger, Jake Gyllenhaal

Doris Day (1924)
Marlon Brando (1924)
Alec Baldwin (1958)

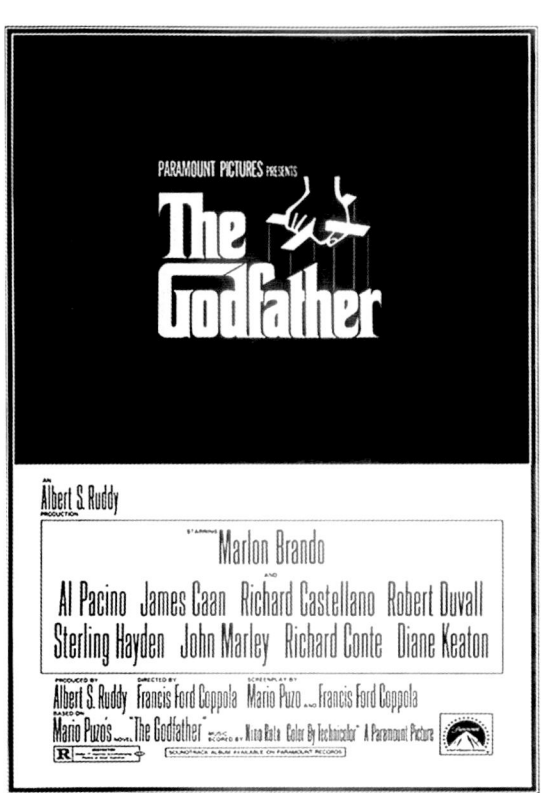

The Godfather

Der Pate / Le Parrain
Francis Ford Coppola, 1972
Robert Duvall, Marlon Brando

X-Men: First Class

X-Men: Erste Entscheidung /
X-Men : Le Commencement
Matthew Vaughn, 2011
Michael Fassbender

"*The Hunchback of Notre Dame* is a two-hour nightmare. It's murderous, hideous and repulsive."

Variety

The Hunchback of Notre Dame

Der Glöckner von Notre Dame / Notre-Dame de Paris
Wallace Worsley, 1923
Lon Chaney

The Tin Drum

Die Blechtrommel / Le Tambour
Volker Schlöndorff, 1979
David Bennent

The Seven Year Itch

Das verflixte 7. Jahr /
Sept ans de réflexion
Billy Wilder, 1955
Marilyn Monroe, Tom Ewell

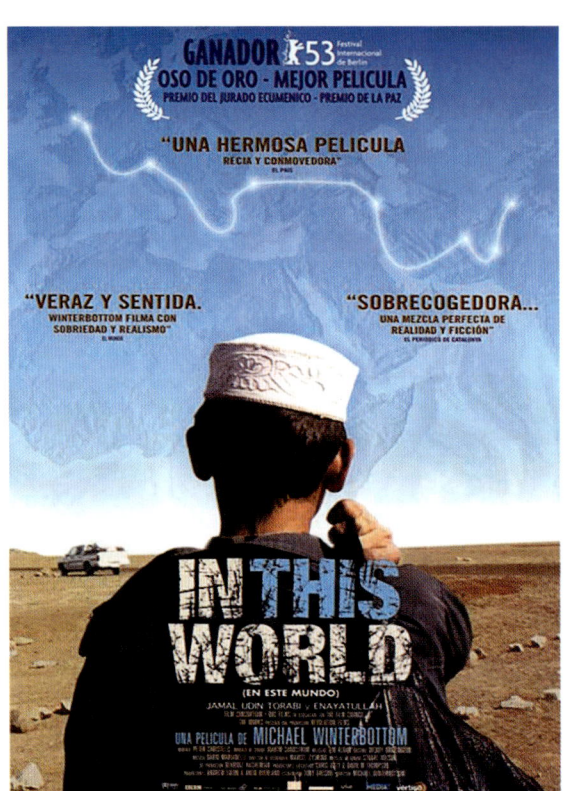

In This World

Michael Winterbottom, 2002
Enayatullah, Jamal Udin Torabi

Dirk Bogarde (1921)
Dianne Wiest (1948)

"WARNING! *Strait-Jacket* vividly depicts ax murders!"

Strait-Jacket

Die Zwangsjacke / La Meurtrière diabolique
William Castle, 1964
Joan Crawford

Inglourious Basterds

Quentin Tarantino, 2009
Christoph Waltz

James Caan (1940)
Keira Knightley (1985)

"The first sound we hear in *Atonement*
is the tap of typewriter keys. Soon, the
tapping becomes regular, like drum-
beats. Later in the film, it rings out as
loudly as gunshots. The implication
is clear: words can stir us and see us
dancing, but they can also kill."

The New Yorker

Atonement

Abbitte / Reviens-moi
Joe Wright, 2007
Keira Knightley

The Ten Commandments

Die Zehn Gebote / Les Dix Commandements
Cecil B. DeMille, 1923
Theodore Roberts

Alfred Hitchcock (1899)

"The Hitchcock touch had four hands, and two were Alma's."

Charles Champlin

Alma Hitchcock

Steve Martin (1945)
Wim Wenders (1945)
Halle Berry (1966)

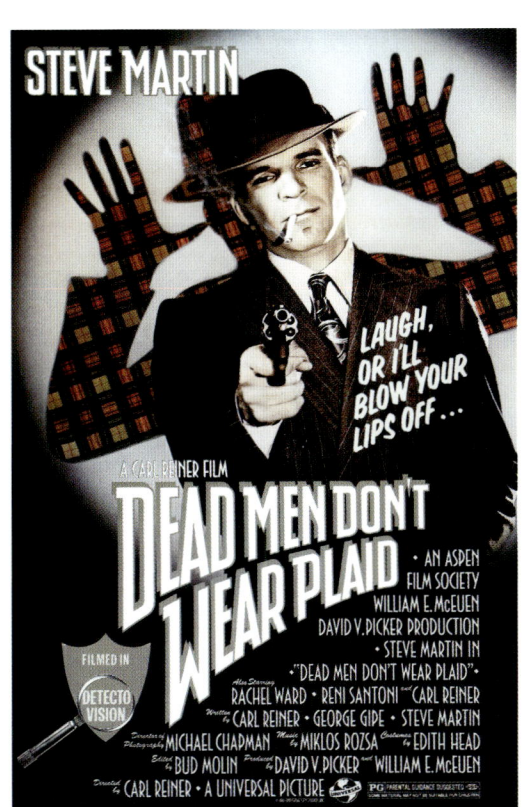

Dead Men Don't Wear Plaid

Tote tragen keine Karos / Les Cadavres
ne portent pas de costard
Carl Reiner, 1981
Steve Martin

Alejandro González Iñárritu (1963)
Jennifer Lawrence (1990)

"I don't care about the chronological order of the facts but rather the emotional impact of the events, because after all is said and done, cinema is just an emotional experience."

Alejandro González Iñárritu

Babel

Alejandro González Iñárritu, 2006
Adriana Barraza

Avatar

Avatar – Aufbruch nach Pandora
James Cameron, 2009
Sam Worthington

Dead Man Walking

La Dernière Marche
Tim Robbins, 1995
Sean Penn

"I'm with you because I choose to be with you. I don't want to live someone else's idea of how to live. Don't ask me to do that."

Denys (Robert Redford)

Out of Africa

Jenseits von Afrika
Sydney Pollack, 1985
Meryl Streep, Robert Redford

Out of the Past

Goldenes Gift / La Griffe du passé
Jacques Tourneur, 1947
Kirk Douglas, Robert Mitchum

That Touch of Mink

Ein Hauch von Nerz /
Un soupçon de vision
Delbert Mann, 1962
Cary Grant, Doris Day

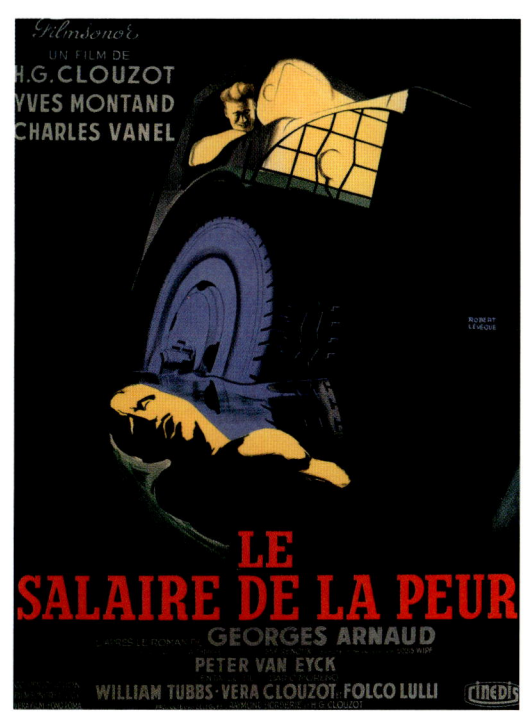

The Wages of Fear

Lohn der Angst / Le Salaire de la peur
Henri-Georges Clouzot, 1953
Peter van Eyck

**Olympia Part One:
Festival of the Nations**

*Olympia 1. Teil: Fest der Völker / Les Dieux
du stade, la fête des peuples*
Leni Riefenstahl, 1936
Robert Clark

Gene Kelly (1912)
Park Chan-wook (1963)

"I'm not a psy-cho. I'm a cy-borg."

Cha Young-goon (Lim Soo-jung)

I'm a Cyborg, But That's OK

Ich bin ein Cyborg, aber das macht nichts /
Je suis un cyborg
Park Chan-wook, 2006
Lim Soo-jung

Born on the Fourth of July

Geboren am 4. Juli / Né un 4 juillet
Oliver Stone, 1989
Tom Cruise, Willem Dafoe

Georg Wilhelm Pabst (1885)
Sean Connery (1930)
Tim Burton (1958)
Sönke Wortmann (1959)
Fatih Akin (1973)

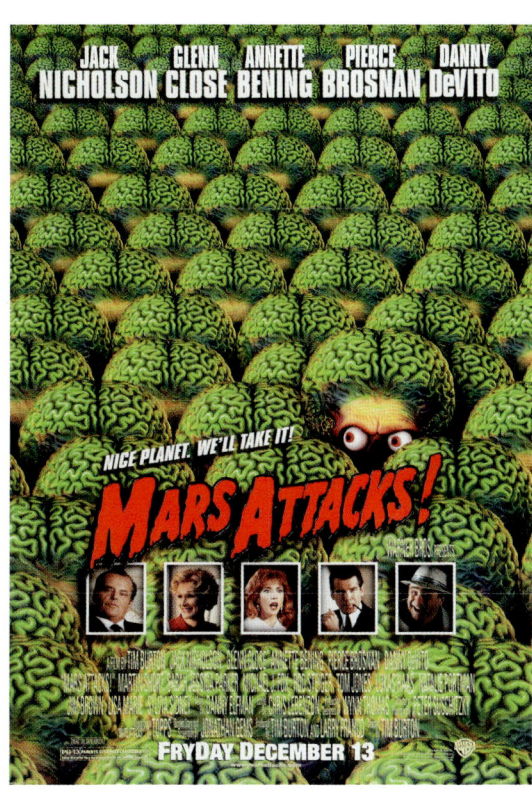

Mars Attacks!

Tim Burton, 1996
Lisa Marie

"When I grow up and get married, I'm living alone."

Kevin (Macaulay Culkin)

Home Alone

Kevin – Allein zu Haus / Maman, j'ai raté l'avion !
Chris Columbus, 1990
Macaulay Culkin

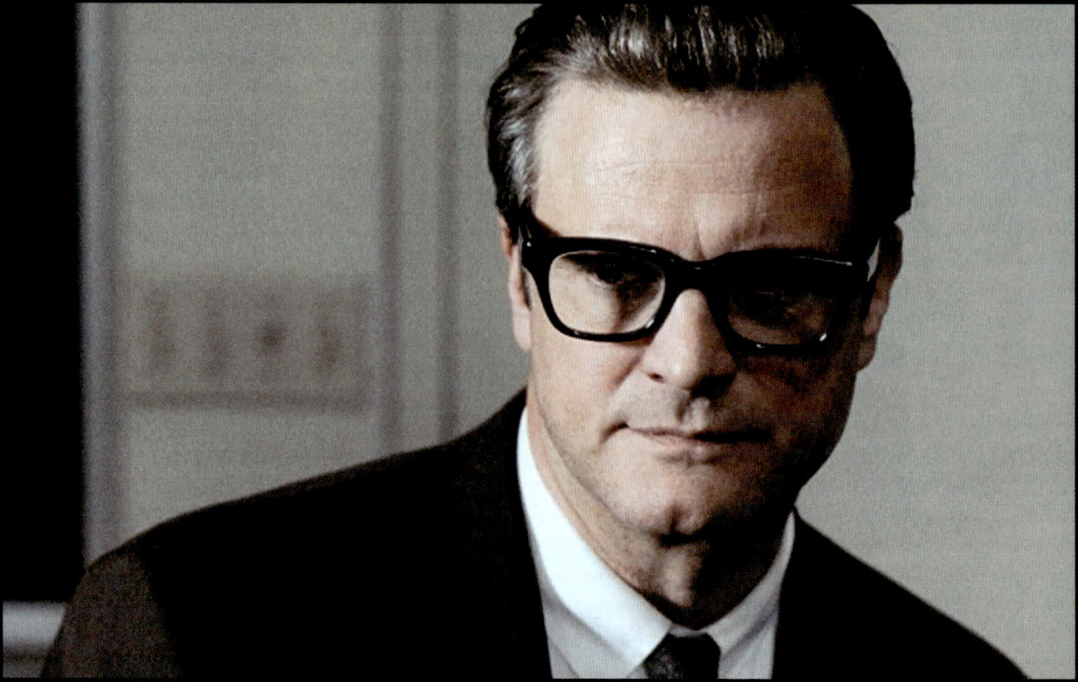

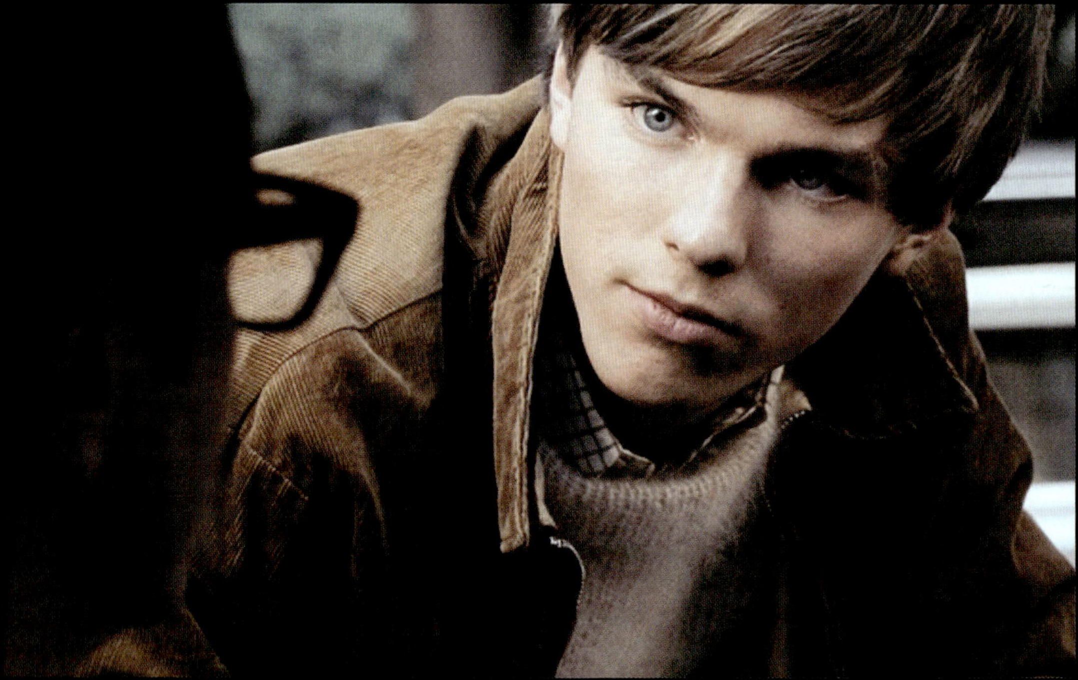

"Tom Ford is the real deal."

The Times

A Single Man

Tom Ford, 2009
Colin Firth, Nicholas Hoult

Se7en

Sieben / Seven
David Fincher, 1995
John C. McGinley

Preston Sturges (1898)
Ingrid Bergman (1915)
Richard Attenborough (1923)

Phantom Lady

Zeuge gesucht / Les mains qui tuent
Robert Siodmak, 1944
Thomas Gomez, Ella Raines,
Franchot Tone

On the set of
Bluebeard's Eighth Wife

Blaubarts achte Frau /
La Huitième Femme de Barbe-Bleue
Ernst Lubitsch, 1938
Gary Cooper, Claudette Colbert,
Ernst Lubitsch

Fredric March (1897)
James Coburn (1928)
Richard Gere (1949)

My Darling Clementine

Faustrecht der Prärie / La Poursuite infernale
John Ford, 1946
Henry Fonda

"Bibbidi-bobbidi-boo."

Fairy Godmother

Cinderella

Aschenputtel / Cendrillon
Clyde Geronimi, 1950

Point Blank

Le Point de non-retour
John Boorman, 1967
Lee Marvin

Amélie

Die fabelhafte Welt der Amélie /
Le fabuleux destin d'Amélie Poulain
Jean-Pierre Jeunet, 2001
Audrey Tautou

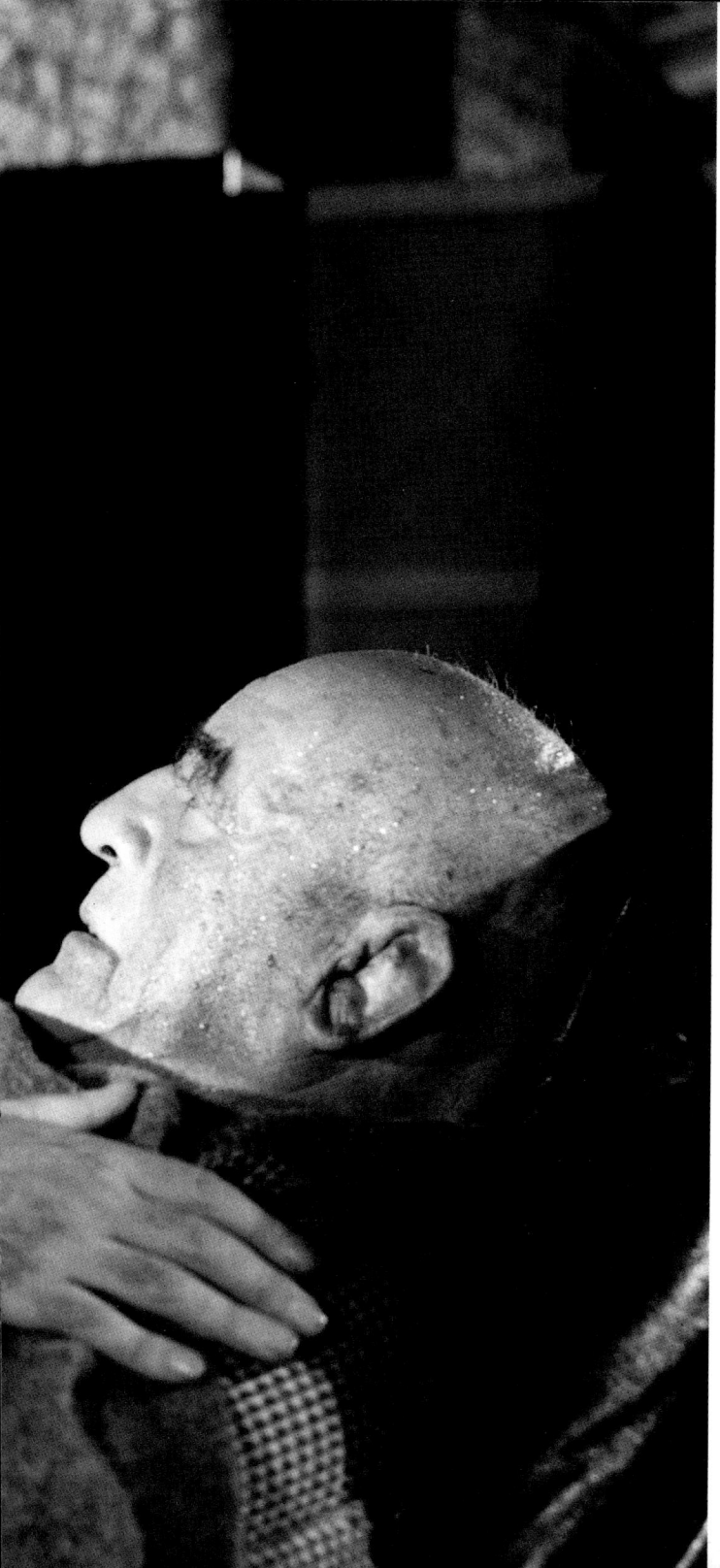

Night and the City

Die Ratte von Soho /
Les Forbans de la nuit
Jules Dassin, 1950
Herbert Lom, Stanislaus Zbyszko

"Werner Herzog's *Fitzcarraldo* is a movie in the great tradition of grandiose cinematic visions. Like Coppola's *Apocalypse Now* or Kubrick's *2001: A Space Odyssey*, it is a quest film in which the hero's quest is scarcely more mad than the filmmaker's."

Roger Ebert

Fitzcarraldo

Werner Herzog, 1981
Klaus Kinski

"This first important film of the vampire genre has more spectral atmosphere, more ingenuity, and more imaginative ghoulish ghastliness than any of its successors."

Pauline Kael

Nosferatu

Nosferatu, eine Symphonie des Grauens /
Nosferatu le vampire
F. W. Murnau, 1922
Max Schreck

A Streetcar Named Desire

Endstation Sehnsucht /
Un tramway nommé Désir
Elia Kazan, 1951
Kim Hunter, Marlon Brando

The Haunting

Bis das Blut gefriert / La Maison du diable
Robert Wise, 1963
Richard Johnson, Julie Harris

"Rita Hayworth used to say: 'They go to bed with Gilda; they wake up with me.'"

Anna Scott (Julia Roberts)

Notting Hill

Coup de foudre à Notting Hill
Roger Michell, 1999
Hugh Grant, Julia Roberts

"A powerful, slow-burning portrait of human fallibility."

Variety

Where the Truth Lies

Wahre Lügen / La Vérité nue
Atom Egoyan, 2005
Alison Lohman, Colin Firth

Foreign Intrigue

Die fünfte Kolonne / L'Enigmatique Monsieur D…
Sheldon Reynolds, 1956
Robert Mitchum

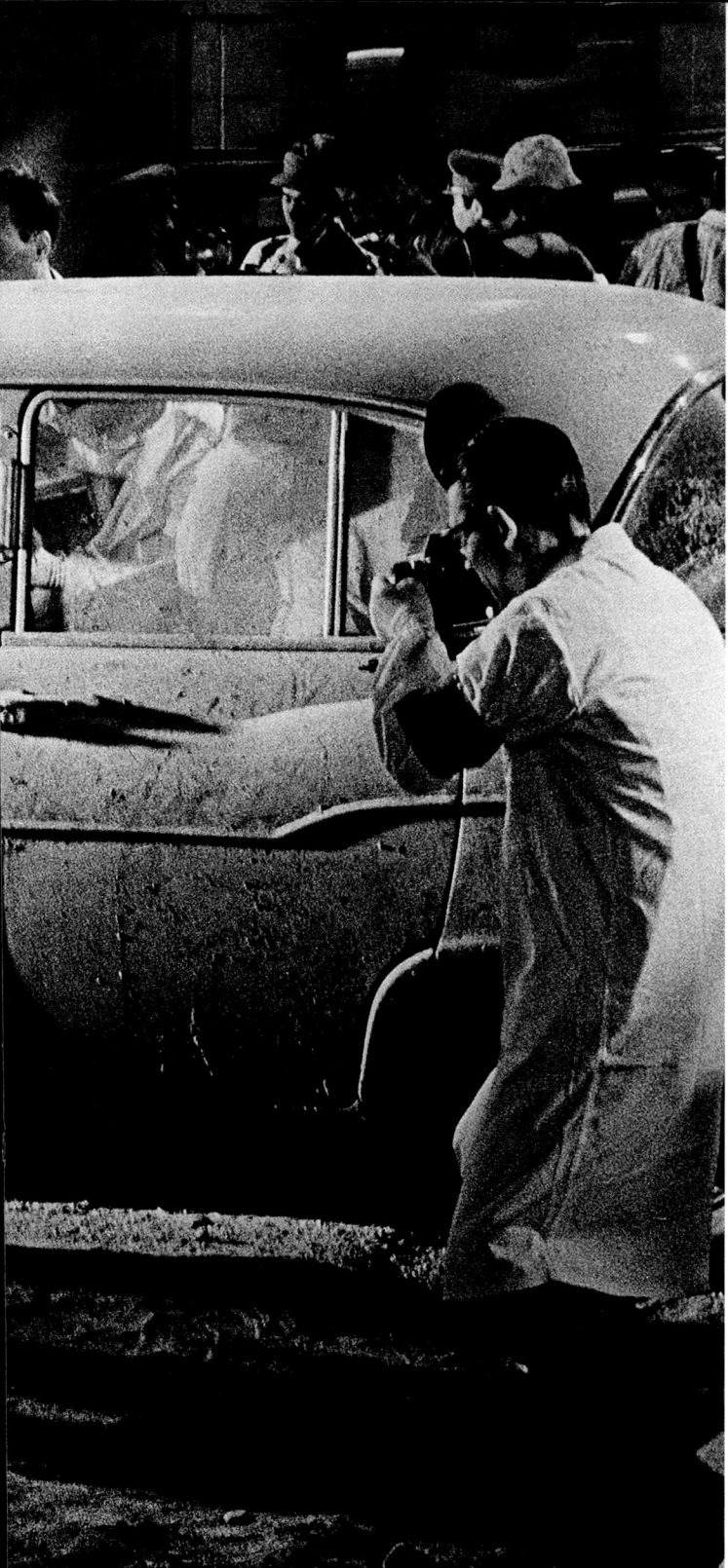

High and Low

Zwischen Himmel und Hölle /
Entre le ciel et l'enfer
Akira Kurosawa, 1963
Toshirô Mifune

"This Jack Clayton adaptation of *The Turn of the Screw* is one of the rare pictures that does justice to Henry James. It's beautifully crafted and acted, immaculately shot (by Freddie Francis), and very scary."

Martin Scorsese

The Innocents

Schloss des Schreckens / Les Innocents
Jack Clayton, 1961
Deborah Kerr

"*The Host* is a monster movie, but I wanted to break the rules. I would have hated it if it took half an hour just to see the monster's tail in dark sewage. The monster shows itself early on — it's what happens next that is important."

Bong Joon-ho

The Host

Bong Joon-ho, 2006
Bae Doo-na

Volver

Volver – Zurückkehren
Pedro Almodóvar, 2006
Carmen Maura, Penélope Cruz

Goldfinger

Guy Hamilton, 1964
Shirley Eaton

Anne Bancroft (1931)
Baz Luhrmann (1962)

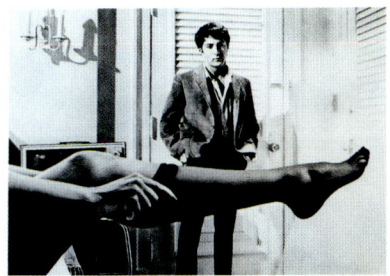

JOSEPH E. LEVINE
MIKE NICHOLS
LAWRENCE TURMAN

This
is
Benjamin.

He's
a little
worried
about
his
future.

THE GRADUATE

ANNE BANCROFT AND DUSTIN HOFFMAN · KATHARINE ROSS
CALDER WILLINGHAM AND BUCK HENRY   PAUL SIMON
SIMON AND GARFUNKEL   LAWRENCE TURMAN
MIKE NICHOLS TECHNICOLOR® PANAVISION®

United Artists

The Graduate

Die Reifeprüfung / Le Lauréat
Mike Nichols, 1967
Anne Bancroft

Greta Garbo (1905)
Robert Blake (1933)
Alison Lohman (1979)

"One can feel nostalgia for places one has never seen."

Queen Christina (Greta Garbo)

Queen Christina

Königin Christine / La Reine Christine
Rouben Mamoulian, 1933
Greta Garbo

"A Monster Science Created — But Could Not Destroy!"

Frankenstein

James Whale, 1931
Boris Karloff

Upton Sinclair (1878)
Victor Sjöström (1879)
Fernando Rey (1917)
Sophia Loren (1934)

The Discreet Charm of the Bourgeoisie

Der diskrete Charme der Bourgeoisie /
Le Charme discret de la bourgeoisie
Luis Buñuel, 1972
Julien Bertheau

"He's having the day of his life ... over and over again."

Groundhog Day

Und täglich grüßt das Murmeltier /
Un jour sans fin
Harold Ramis, 1993
Bill Murray

Erich von Stroheim (1885)
Hans Albers (1891)

Große Freiheit Nr. 7

La Paloma
Helmut Käutner, 1943/44
Hans Albers

"Do you still need a corpse?
Here comes one now!"

Abbott & Costello Meet Frankenstein

Abbott und Costello treffen Frankenstein /
Deux nigauds contre Frankenstein
Charles T. Barton, 1948
Lon Chaney Jr.

SEPTEMBER 24

Pedro Almodóvar (1949)

On the set of
Bad Education

*La mala educación – Schlechte
Erziehung / La Mauvaise Éducation*
Pedro Almodóvar, 2004
Pedro Almodóvar, Gael García Bernal

Michael Douglas (1944)
Christopher Reeve (1952)
Catherine Zeta-Jones (1969)

"To commit the crime of the century, a man naturally wants to face the challenge of the century."

Lex Luthor (Gene Hackman)

Superman

Richard Donner, 1978
Christopher Reeve

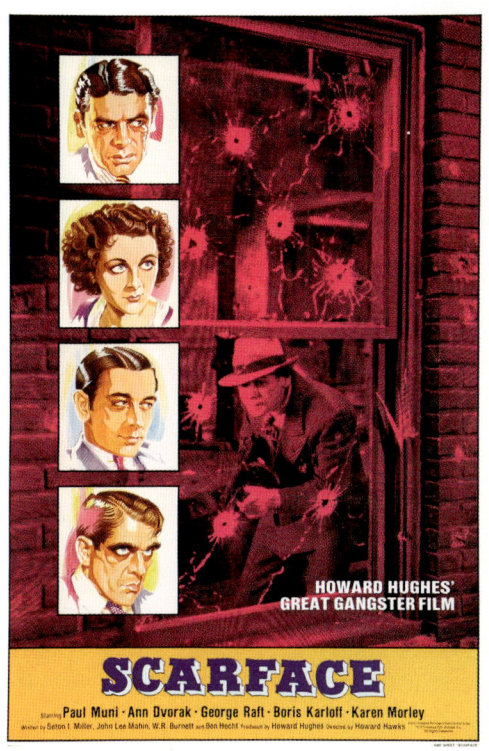

Scarface

Howard Hawks, 1932
Paul Muni

Arthur Penn (1922)
Gwyneth Paltrow (1972)

Shakespeare in Love

John Madden, 1998
Gwyneth Paltrow

Mulholland Drive

David Lynch, 2001
Naomi Watts

Michelangelo Antonioni (1912)
Anita Ekberg (1931)
Nicolas Winding Refn (1970)

La Dolce Vita

Das süße Leben
Federico Fellini, 1959
Anita Ekberg

Deborah Kerr (1921)
Truman Capote (1924)
Monica Bellucci (1964)
Marion Cotillard (1975)

"No witnesses!"

Richard "Dick" Hickock (Scott Wilson)

In Cold Blood

Kaltblütig / De sang-froid
Richard Brooks, 1967
Scott Wilson

Walter Matthau (1920)
Julie Andrews (1935)
Jean-Jacques Annaud (1943)

The Sound of Music

Meine Lieder, meine Träume /
La Mélodie du bonheur
Robert Wise, 1965
Julie Andrews

Groucho Marx (1890)
Bud Abbott (1895)

A Night in Casablanca

Eine Nacht in Casablanca /
Une nuit à Casablanca
Archie Mayo, 1946
Groucho Marx, Chico Marx,
Harpo Marx, Lisette Verea

**"I wanted to make a film that
when the final credits roll . . .
that's really the beginning of the film."**

Alfonso Cuarón

Children of Men

Les Fils de l'homme
Alfonso Cuarón, 2006
Clive Owen

The General

Der General / Le Mécano de la "General"
Buster Keaton, 1926/27
Buster Keaton

Louis Lumière (1864)
Guy Pearce (1967)
Kate Winslet (1975)

"It doesn't matter what I feel. It doesn't matter what I think. The dead are still dead."

Hanna Schmitz (Kate Winslet)

The Reader

Der Vorleser
Stephen Daldry, 2008
Kate Winslet

Janet Gaynor (1906)
Carole Lombard (1908)

To Be or Not to Be

Sein oder Nichtsein / Jeux dangereux
Ernst Lubitsch, 1942
Carole Lombard, Jack Benny

"Like all art forms, film is
a medium as powerful as weapons
of mass destruction; the only
difference is that war destroys
and film inspires."

Nicolas Winding Refn

Pusher II

Pusher II: Respect /
Pusher II – Du sang sur les mains
Nicolas Winding Refn, 2004
Mads Mikkelsen

Sigourney Weaver (1949)
Matt Damon (1970)

"When you double-cross a double-crosser ... IT'S A CRISS-CROSS!"

Criss Cross

Gewagtes Alibi / Pour toi j'ai tué
Robert Siodmak, 1949
Yvonne De Carlo, Burt Lancaster

Pan's Labyrinth

Pans Labyrinth / Le Labyrinthe de Pan
Guillermo Del Toro, 2006
Doug Jones, Ivana Baquero

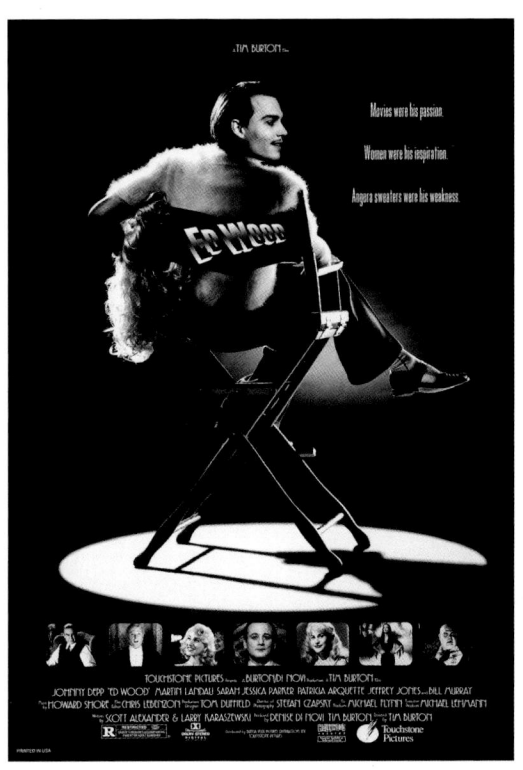

Ed Wood

Tim Burton, 1994
Johnny Depp, Martin Landau

Joan Cusack (1962)
Takeshi Kaneshiro (1973)

"Dreamy and creepy, tender and terrifying, *Somersault* is a frank and visceral film that at the same time exudes an unexpected innocence."

Los Angeles Times

Somersault

Somersault – Wie Parfum in der Luft
Cate Shortland, 2004
Abbie Cornish

OCTOBER 12

Hugh Jackman (1968)

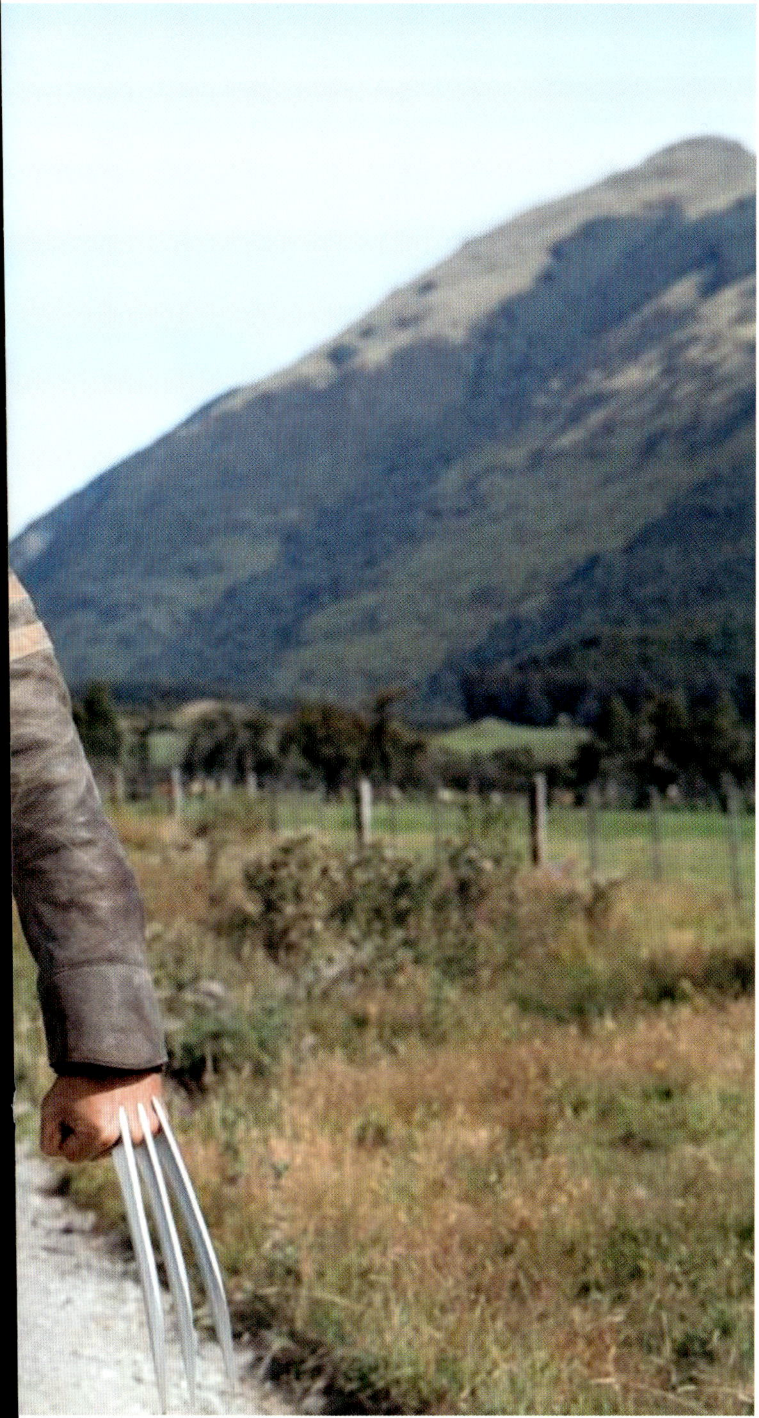

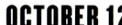

X-Men Origins: Wolverine

Gavin Hood, 2009
Hugh Jackman

Robert Walker (1918)
Yves Montand (1921)
Sacha Baron Cohen (1971)

"Please, you come see my film . . .
If it not success, I will be execute."

Borat (Sacha Baron Cohen)

Borat

Larry Charles, 2006
Sacha Baron Cohen

Lillian Gish (1893)
Roger Moore (1927)
Udo Kier (1944)

The Night of the Hunter

Die Nacht des Jägers / La Nuit du chasseur
Charles Laughton, 1955
Robert Mitchum, Sally Jane Bruce

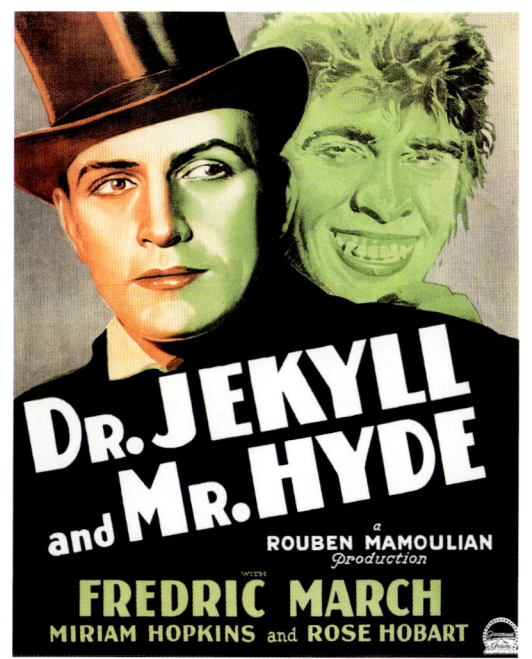

Dr. Jekyll and Mr. Hyde

Dr. Jekyll und Mr. Hyde /
Docteur Jekyll et M. Hyde
Rouben Mamoulian, 1931
Miriam Hopkins, Fredric March

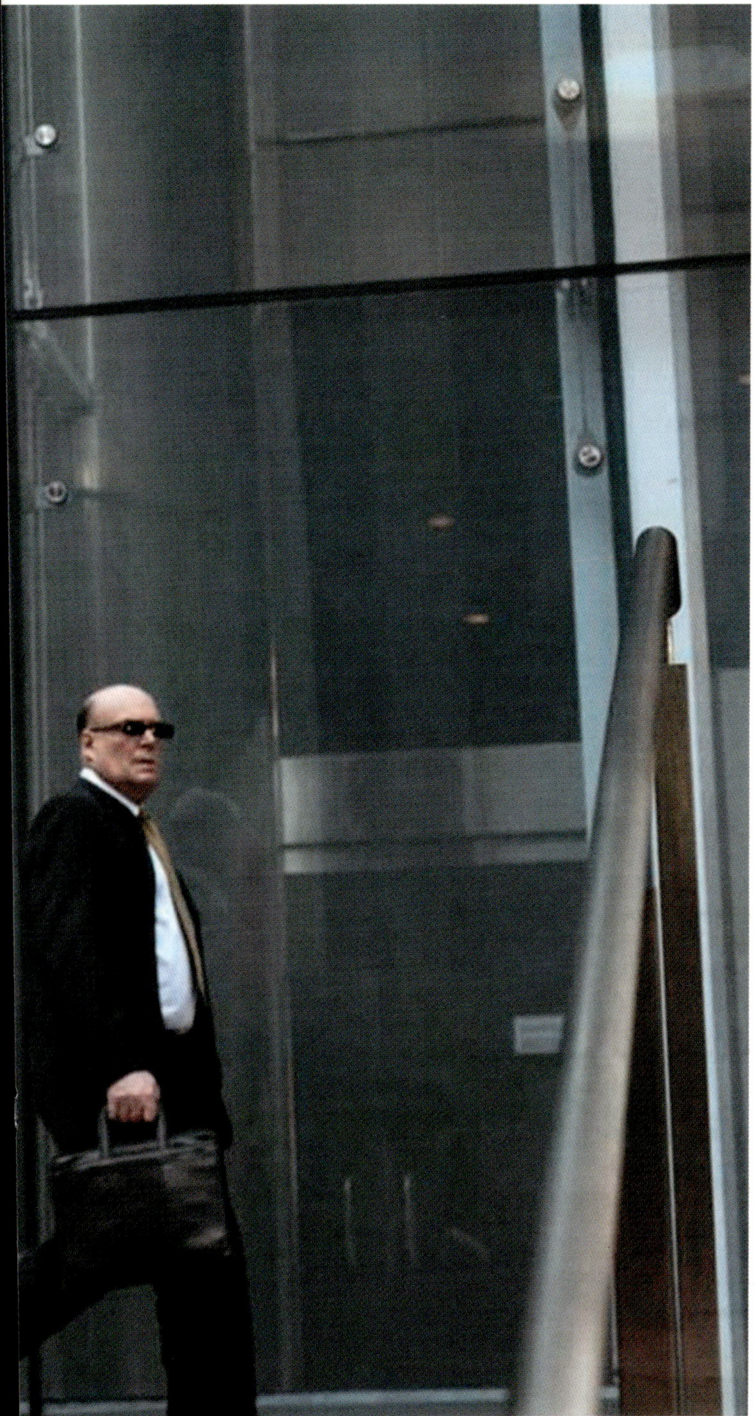

OCTOBER 16

Tim Robbins (1958)

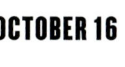

The Social Network

David Fincher, 2010
Jesse Eisenberg

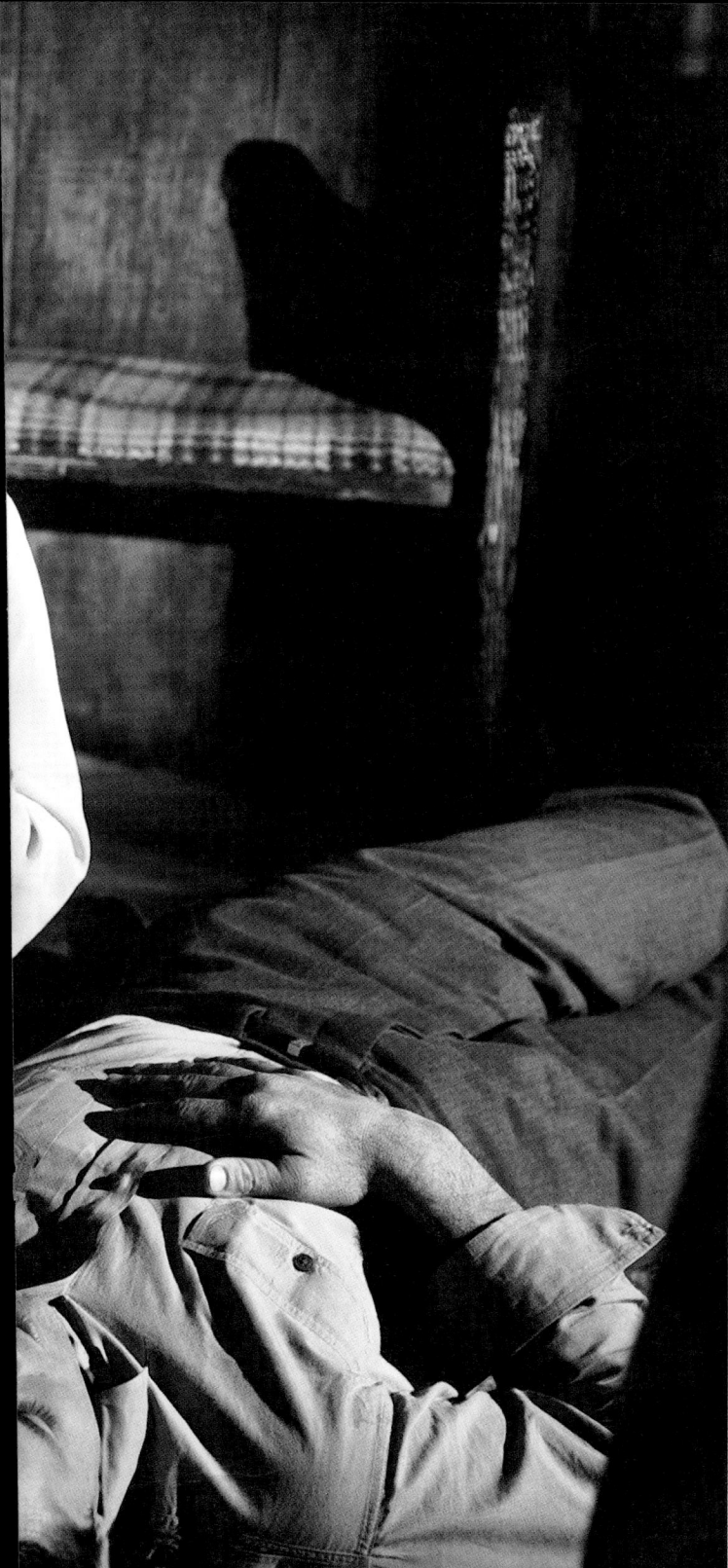

Love Letters

Liebesbriefe / Le Poids d'un mensonge
William Dieterle, 1945
Jennifer Jones, Robert Sully

Klaus Kinski (1926)
George C. Scott (1927)
Peter Boyle (1935)
Jean-Claude Van Damme (1960)
Freida Pinto (1984)

"This is one lobster you don't want to order!"

Ebirah, Horror of the Deep

Jun Fukuda, 1966

"It comes straight at you like an arrow — beware!"

Arrival of a Train at La Ciotat

*Die Ankunft eines Zuges auf dem Bahnhof
in La Ciotat / L'Arrivée d'un train en gare
de La Ciotat*
Auguste Lumière, 1895

Bela Lugosi (1882)
Jean-Pierre Melville (1917)
Danny Boyle (1956)
Viggo Mortensen (1958)

"*Eastern Promises* is no ordinary crime thriller, just as Cronenberg is no ordinary director."

Roger Ebert

Eastern Promises

Tödliche Versprechen / Les Promesses de l'ombre
David Cronenberg, 2007
Viggo Mortensen

Carrie Fisher (1956)
Ken Watanabe (1959)

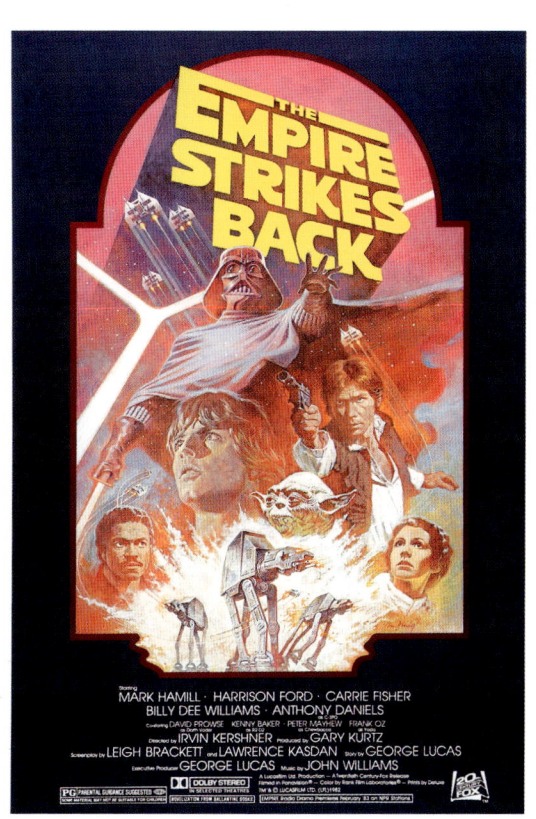

The Empire Strikes Back

Das Imperium schlägt zurück / Star Wars,
épisode V : L'Empire contre-attaque
Irvin Kershner, 1979
Frank Oz

Belle de Jour

Belle de Jour – Schöne des Tages
Luis Buñuel, 1966
Catherine Deneuve

OCTOBER 23

Gummo Marx (1892)
Michael Crichton (1942)
Ang Lee (1954)

Crouching Tiger, Hidden Dragon

Tiger & Dragon / Tigre & Dragon
Ang Lee, 2000
Zhang Ziyi

Merian C. Cooper (1893)
F. Murray Abraham (1939)
Kevin Kline (1947)

King Kong

King Kong und die weiße Frau
Merian C. Cooper, Ernest B. Schoedsack,
1933
Fay Wray, Robert Armstrong

"In the shadow of this ambiguous giant called China, what does it mean to be a Hong Kongese?"

Johnnie To

Exiled

Exilé
Johnnie To, 2006
Francis Ng, Roy Cheung,
Anthony Wong, Lam Suet

Mildred Pierce

*Solange ein Herz schlägt / Le Roman de
Mildred Pierce*
Michael Curtiz, 1945
Jack Carson, Zachary Scott

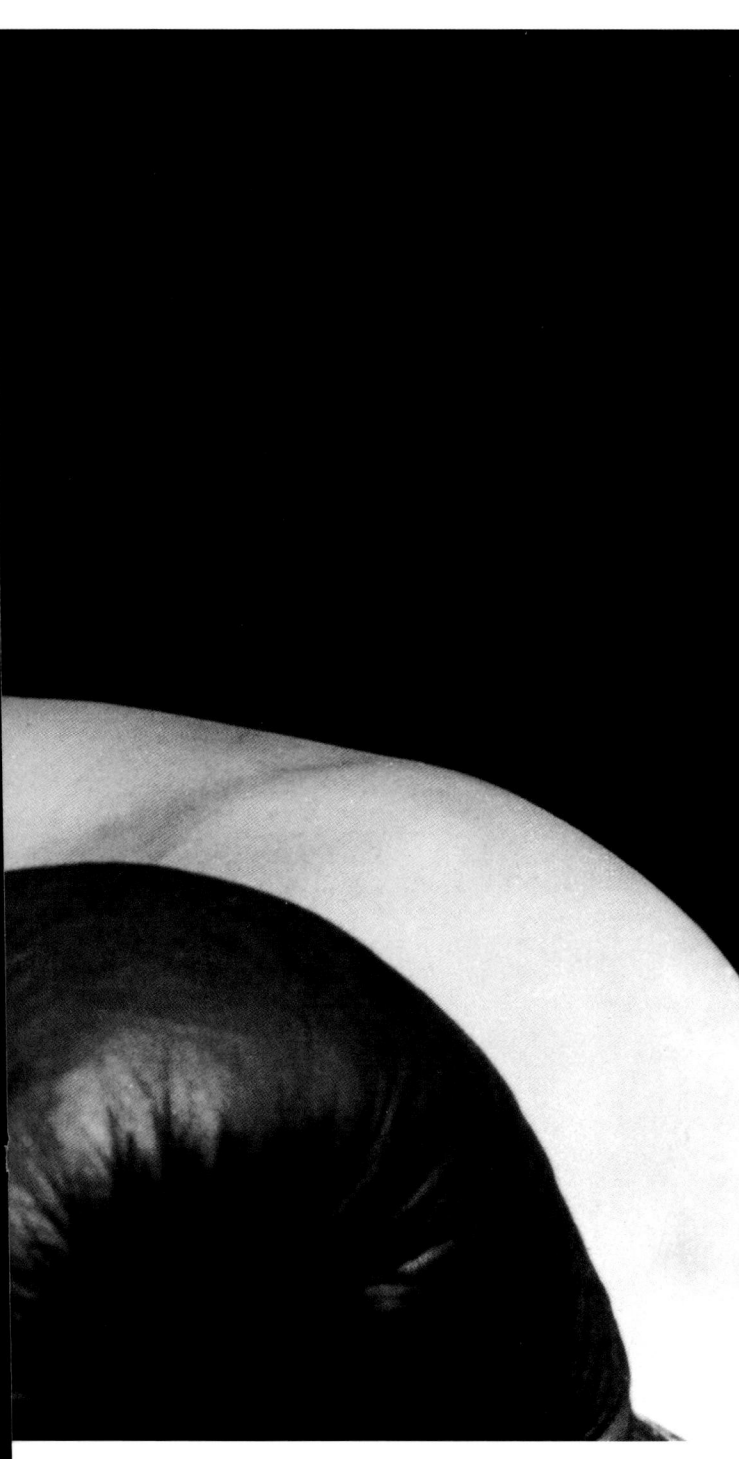

Roberto Benigni (1952)

Champion

Zwischen Frauen und Seilen /
Le Champion
Mark Robson, 1949
Kirk Douglas

Edith Head (1897)
Julia Roberts (1967)
Joaquin Phoenix (1974)

"Love is a burning thing."

Johnny Cash, "Ring of Fire"

Walk the Line

James Mangold, 2005
Joaquin Phoenix, Reese Witherspoon

Eddie Constantine (1913)
Winona Ryder (1971)

The Asphalt Jungle

Asphalt Dschungel / Quand la ville dort
John Huston, 1950
Anthony Caruso, Sterling Hayden

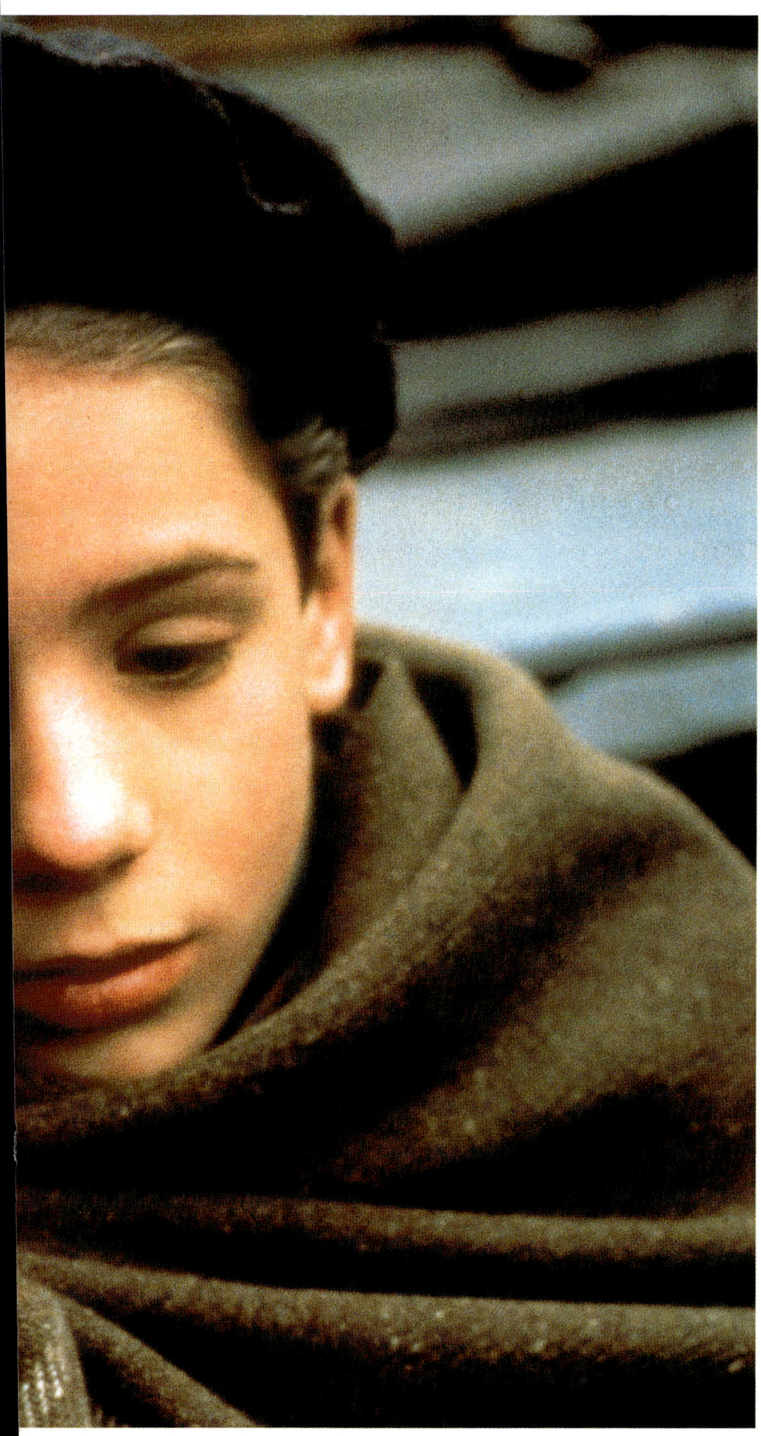

OCTOBER 30

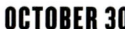

Ruth Gordon (1896)
Louis Malle (1932)

Au revoir les enfants

Auf Wiedersehen, Kinder
Louis Malle, 1987
Raphaël Fejtö, Gaspard Manesse

An Education

Une éducation
Lone Scherfig, 2009
Peter Sarsgaard, Carey Mulligan

**"It is Coppola's most lavish and, cer-
tainly, his most flamboyant film;
never before has he allowed himself
this kind of mad experimentation."**

The Washington Post

Bram Stoker's Dracula

Francis Ford Coppola, 1992
Gary Oldman, Florina Kendrick,
Michaela Bercu, Monica Bellucci

Luchino Visconti (1906)
Burt Lancaster (1913)
Shah Rukh Khan (1965)

Force of Evil

L'Enfer de la corruption
Abraham Polonsky, 1948
John Garfield, Marie Windsor

Charles Bronson (1921)
Dolph Lundgren (1957)

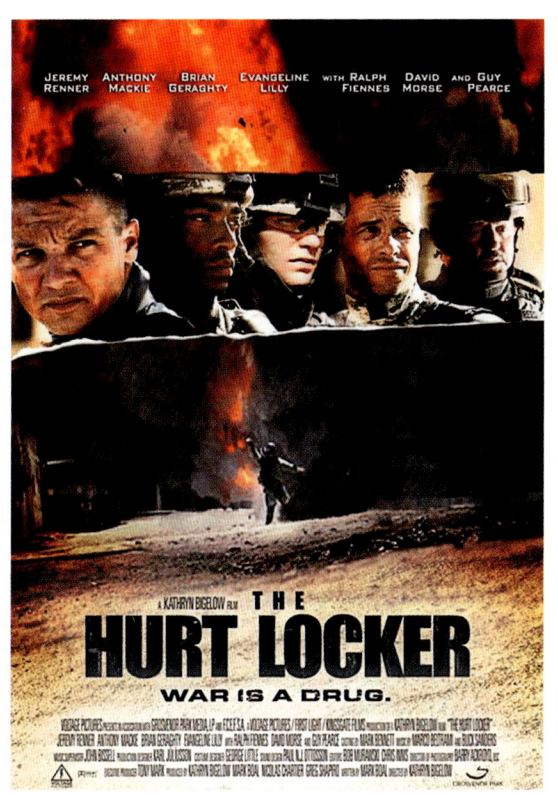

The Hurt Locker

Tödliches Kommando – The Hurt Locker /
Démineurs
Kathryn Bigelow, 2008
Jeremy Renner

Pickup on South Street

Polizei greift ein / Le Port de la drogue
Samuel Fuller, 1953
Jean Peters, Richard Widmark

Gone with the Wind

Vom Winde verweht / Autant en emporte le vent
Victor Fleming, 1939
Vivien Leigh

Cover Girl

Es tanzt die Göttin / La Reine de Broadway
Charles Vidor, 1944
Rita Hayworth, Phil Silvers

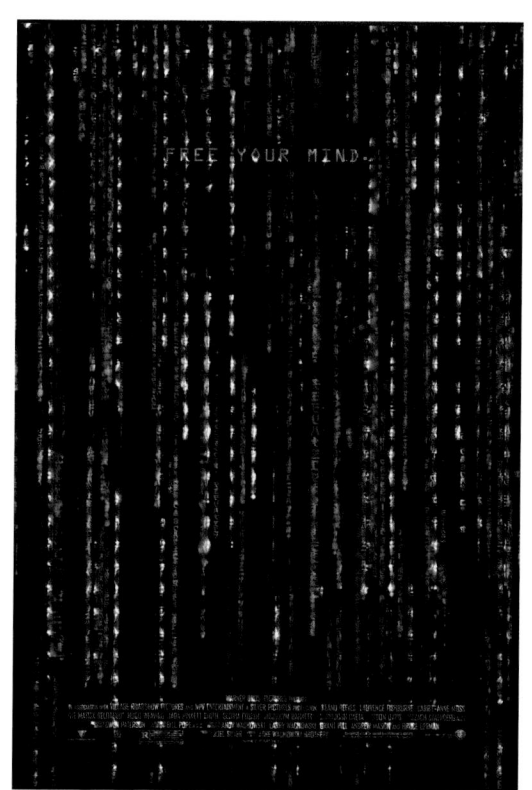

The Matrix Reloaded

Matrix Reloaded
Andy Wachowski, Lana Wachowski, 2002
Carrie-Anne Moss, Laurence Fishburne,
Keanu Reeves

"I never lose. Never really."

Jef Costello (Alain Delon)

Le Samouraï

Der eiskalte Engel
Jean-Pierre Melville, 1967
Alain Delon

Ecstasy

Symphonie der Liebe / Extase
Gustav Machatý, 1932/33
Hedy Lamarr, Aribert Mog

Claude Rains (1889)
Richard Burton (1925)
Ennio Morricone (1928)

Once Upon a Time in the West

Spiel mir das Lied vom Tod /
Il était une fois dans l'Ouest
Sergio Leone, 1968
Charles Bronson

René Clair (1898)
Bibi Andersson (1935)
Leonardo DiCaprio (1974)

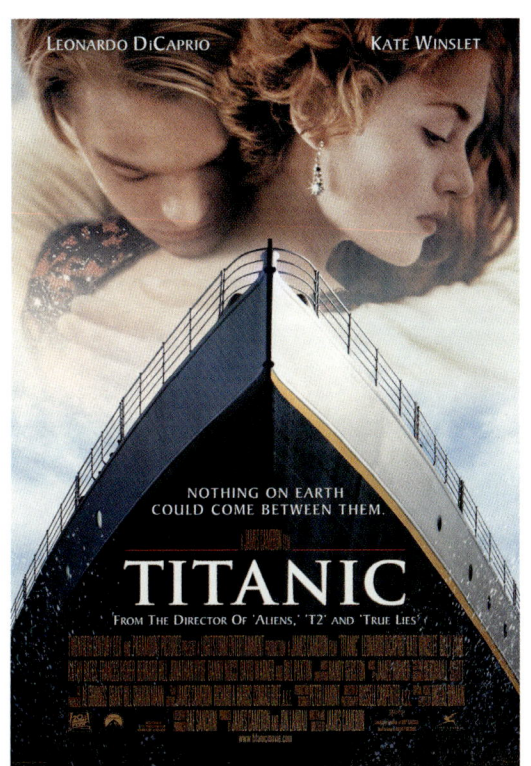

Titanic

James Cameron, 1997
Leonardo DiCaprio, Kate Winslet

Drive

Nicolas Winding Refn, 2011
Ryan Gosling

Gunnar Björnstrand (1909)
Whoopi Goldberg (1955)
Gerard Butler (1969)

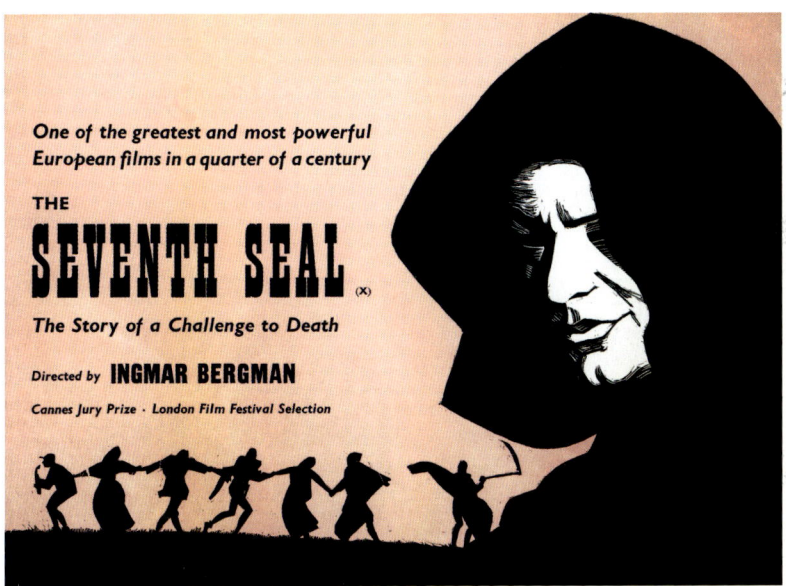

The Seventh Seal

Das siebente Siegel / Le Septième Sceau
Ingmar Bergman, 1956
Bengt Ekerot

Veronica Lake (1922)
Zhang Yimou (1951)

–"I want this picture to be a document. I want to hold a mirror up to life. I want this to be a picture of dignity; a true canvas of the suffering of humanity!"
–"But with a little sex in it."

John L. Sullivan (Joel McCrea) and Mister LeBrand (Robert Warwick)

Sullivan's Travels

Sullivans Reisen / Les Voyages de Sullivan
Preston Sturges, 1941
Joel McCrea, Veronica Lake

"Whatever you call this one-of-a-kind bonbon spiked with wit and malice, it's classic oo-la-la."

Rolling Stone

8 Women

8 Frauen / 8 Femmes
François Ozon, 2001
Catherine Deneuve, Virginie Ledoyen,
Isabelle Huppert, Firmine Richard,
Emanuelle Béart, Fanny Ardant,
Ludivine Sagnier, Danielle Darrieux

Maggie Gyllenhaal (1977)

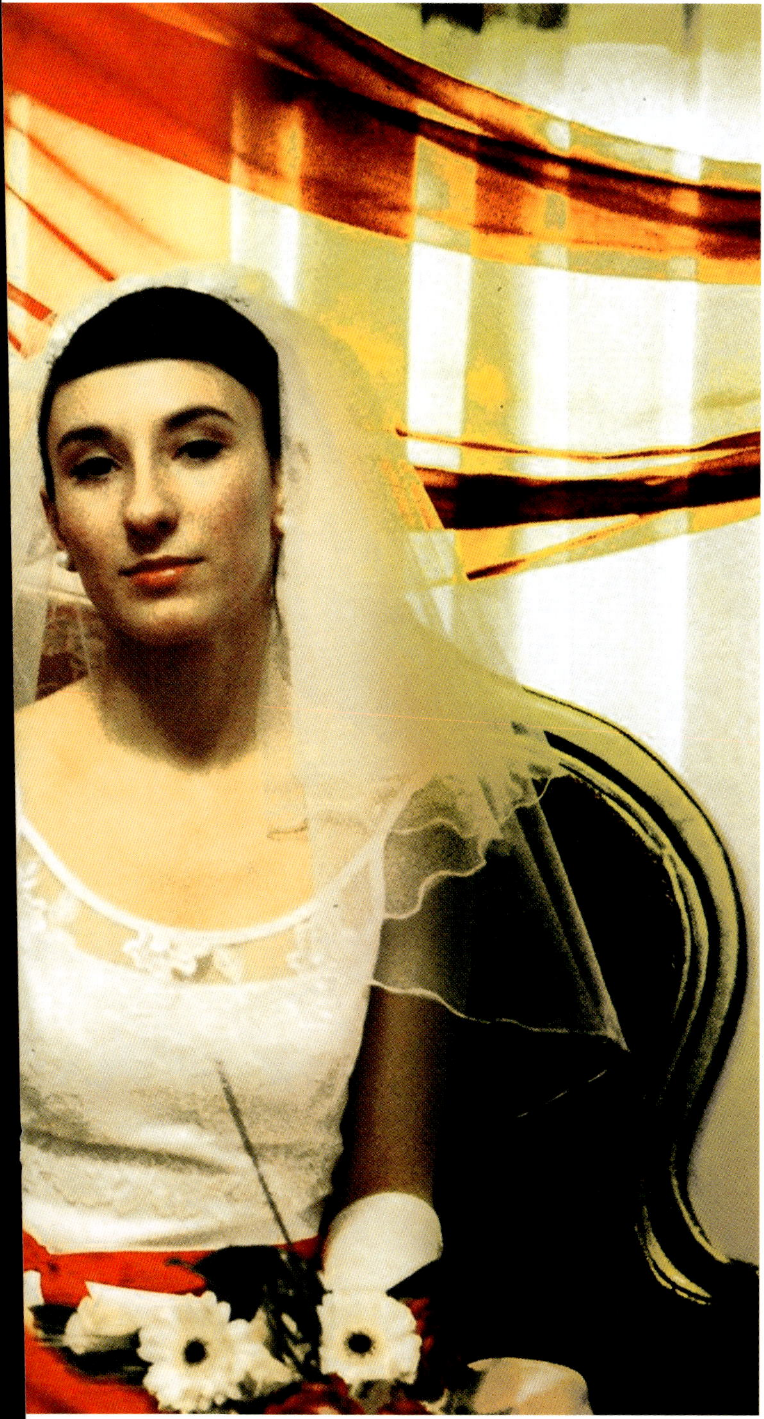

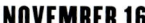

Head-On

Gegen die Wand / Head-On
Fatih Akin, 2003/04
Birol Ünel, Sibel Kekilli

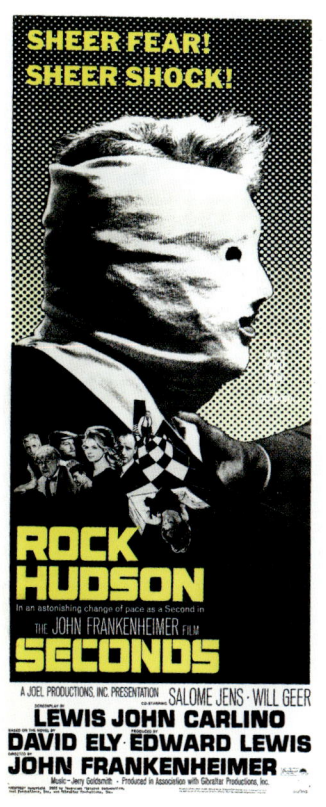

Seconds

*Der Mann, der zweimal lebte /
L'Opération diabolique*
John Frankenheimer, 1966
Rock Hudson, Salome Jens

"I want us to make this trip a spiritual journey where each of us seek the unknown, and we learn about it. Can we agree to that?"

Francis (Owen Wilson)

The Darjeeling Limited

Darjeeling Limited / À bord du Darjeeling Limited
Wes Anderson, 2007
Jason Schwartzman, Owen Wilson,
Adrien Brody

Gene Tierney (1920)
Charlie Kaufman (1958)
Jodie Foster (1962)

The Silence of the Lambs

Das Schweigen der Lämmer /
Le Silence des agneaux
Jonathan Demme, 1991
Jodie Foster

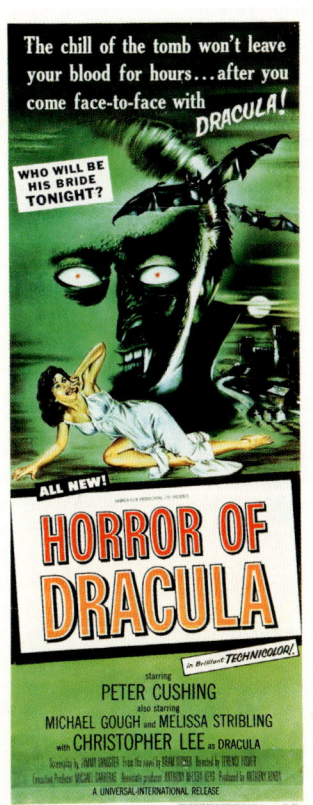

Horror of Dracula

Le Cauchemar de Dracula
Terence Fisher, 1958
Christopher Lee, Melissa Stribling

"Cry — 'God for Harry! England and Saint George!'"

King Henry V (Laurence Olivier)

Henry V

Laurence Olivier, 1944
Laurence Olivier

Terry Gilliam (1940)
Jamie Lee Curtis (1958)
Mads Mikkelsen (1965)
Marjane Satrapi (1969)
Scarlett Johansson (1984)

Persepolis

Vincent Paronnaud, 2006
Marjane Satrapi

Boris Karloff (1887)
Harpo Marx (1888)
Vincent Cassel (1966)

"Don't look now, but there's one man too many in this room, and I think it's you."

Rufus T. Firefly (Groucho Marx)

Duck Soup

Die Marx Brothers im Krieg / La Soupe au canard
Leo McCarey, 1933
Zeppo Marx, Chico Marx,
Groucho Marx, Harpo Marx

Black Cat, White Cat

Schwarze Katze, weißer Kater /
Chat noir, chat blanc
Emir Kusturica, 1998
Branka Katić

Laura

Otto Preminger, 1944
Dana Andrews, Gene Tierney

"*Silent Light* has some sublime, meditative moments: moments of pure, unapologetic visual ecstasy that come close to repealing the cinematic laws of gravity."

The Guardian

Silent Light

Stilles Licht / Lumières silencieuse
Carlos Reygadas, 2007

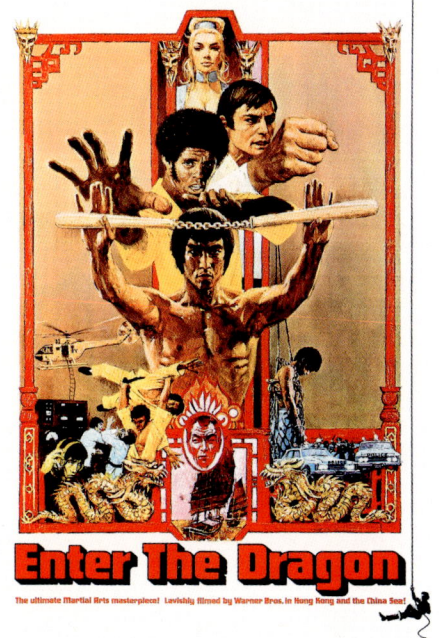

Enter the Dragon

Bruce Lee – Der Mann mit der Todeskralle /
Opération Dragon
Robert Clouse, 1973
Bruce Lee

"Shirô Toyoda ... a master adapter, a true actor's director and one of the Japanese cinema's finest craftsmen."

Donald Richie

The Legend of the White Serpent

Die weiße Schlangenfrau /
La Légende du serpent blanc
Shirô Toyoda, 1956
Ryô Ikebe, Shirley Yamaguchi

"You were right, Garance: love is so simple"

Jean Baptiste Deburau (Jean-Louis Barrault)

Children of Paradise

Kinder des Olymp / Les Enfants du Paradis
Marcel Carné, 1943–45
Jean-Louis Barrault

Ridley Scott (1937)
Terrence Malick (1943)
Gael García Bernal (1978)

"*Blade Runner* was the science fiction of the '80s. The gritty gray counterpart to Kubrick's *2001.*"

epd Film

Blade Runner

Ridley Scott, 1982

**"By day he is Woody Allen. But when
night falls and the moon rises,
Humphrey Bogart strikes again."**

Play It Again, Sam

*Mach's noch einmal, Sam /
Tombe les filles et tais-toi*
Herbert Ross, 1972
Woody Allen

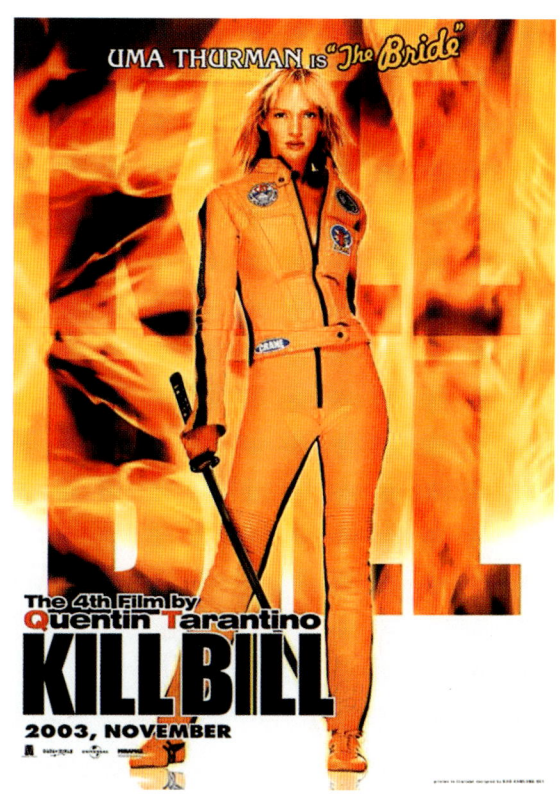

Kill Bill – Volume 1

Quentin Tarantino, 2003/04
Lucy Liu

Far from Heaven

Dem Himmel so fern / Loin du paradis
Todd Haynes, 2002
Julianne Moore

True Grit

Ethan Coen, Joel Coen, 2010
Jeff Bridges

"Congratulations to you, Mickey!"

Leopold Stokowski

Fantasia

Samuel Armstrong, 1940
Mickey Mouse

"If I leave here without understanding you, the world will see you as a monster. I don't want that."

Truman Capote (Philip Seymour Hoffman)

Capote

Truman Capote
Bennett Miller, 2005
Philip Seymour Hoffman

Eli Wallach (1915)
Nicholas Hoult (1989)

The Set-Up

Ring frei für Stoker Thompson /
Nous avons gagné ce soir
Robert Wise, 1949
Robert Ryan, Hal Baylor

Georges Méliès (1861)
Maximilian Schell (1930)
Kim Basinger (1953)

"I'll feed you,
I'll dress you in the morning,
I'll undress you at night ...
I'll take care of you."

John (Mickey Rourke)

9 1/2 Weeks

9 1/2 Wochen / Neuf semaines 1/2
Adrian Lyne, 1985
Kim Basinger

Kirk Douglas (1916)
John Cassavetes (1929)
Judi Dench (1934)
John Malkovich (1953)

"Tell me what you want me to be. How you want me to be. I can be that. I can be anything. Just tell me, Nicky!"

Mabel (Gena Rowlands)

A Woman Under the Influence

Eine Frau unter Einfluss /
Une femme sous influence
John Cassavetes, 1974
Gena Rowlands, Peter Falk

"*The Cremaster Cycle* by Matthew Barney
is the first truly great piece of cinema to
be made in a fine art context since Dalí and
Buñuel filmed *Un Chien Andalou* in 1929."

The Guardian

Cremaster 3

Matthew Barney, 2002
Matthew Barney

Jean Marais (1913)
Jean-Louis Trintignant (1930)

Orpheus

Orphée
Jean Cocteau, 1949
María Casares, Jean Marais

Edward G. Robinson (1893)
Frank Sinatra (1915)

The Killing

Die Rechnung ging nicht auf / L'Ultime Razzia
Stanley Kubrick, 1956
Sterling Hayden

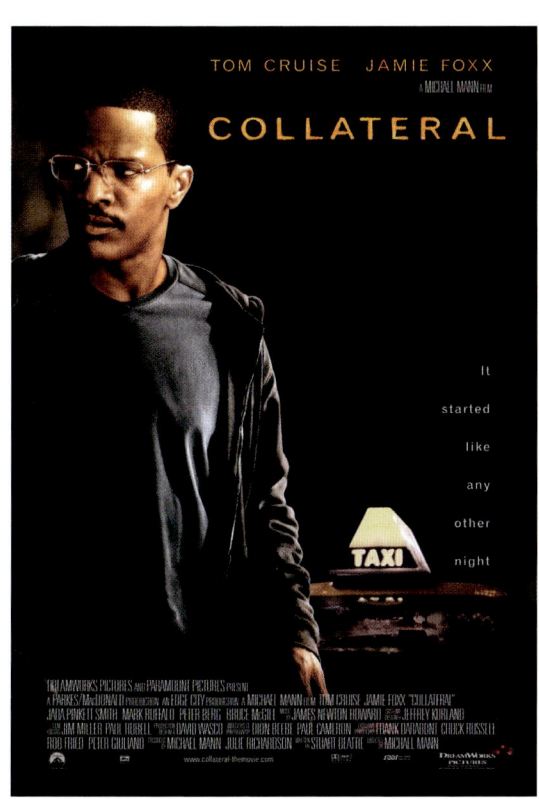

Collateral

Collatéral
Michael Mann, 2004
Tom Cruise, Jamie Foxx

"Kurosawa has always been a director of great images, and in his old age he has permitted himself more fanciful, less realistic ones."

Roger Ebert

Rhapsody in August

Rhapsodie im August / Rhapsodie en août
Akira Kurosawa, 1991
Sachiko Murase

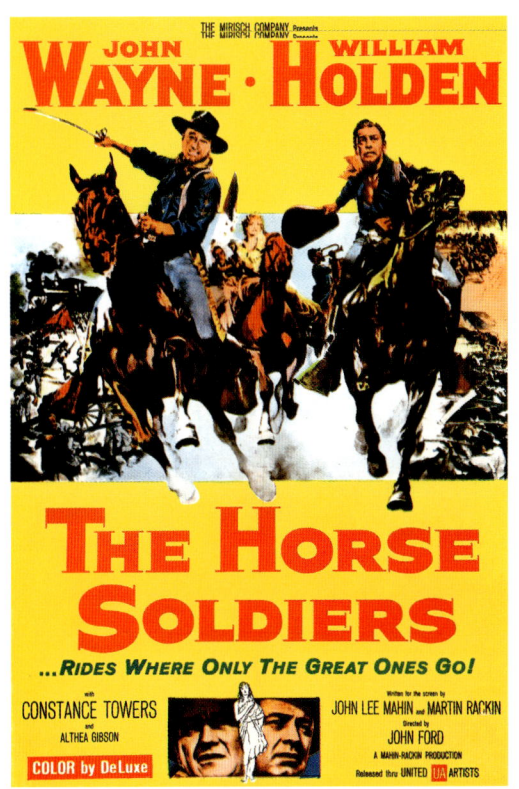

The Horse Soldiers

Der letzte Befehl / Les Cavaliers
John Ford, 1959
John Wayne

Persona

Ingmar Bergman, 1966
Liv Ullmann

Armin Müller-Stahl (1930)
Milla Jovovich (1975)

"A little knowledge can be a deadly thing"

The Man Who Knew Too Much

Der Mann, der zuviel wusste /
L'Homme qui en savait trop
Alfred Hitchcock, 1956
Christopher Olsen

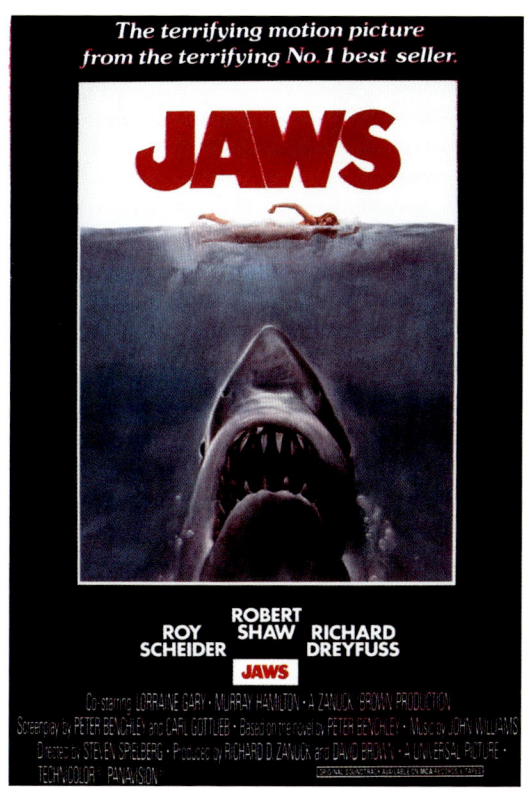

Jaws

Der weiße Hai / Les Dents de la mer
Steven Spielberg, 1975

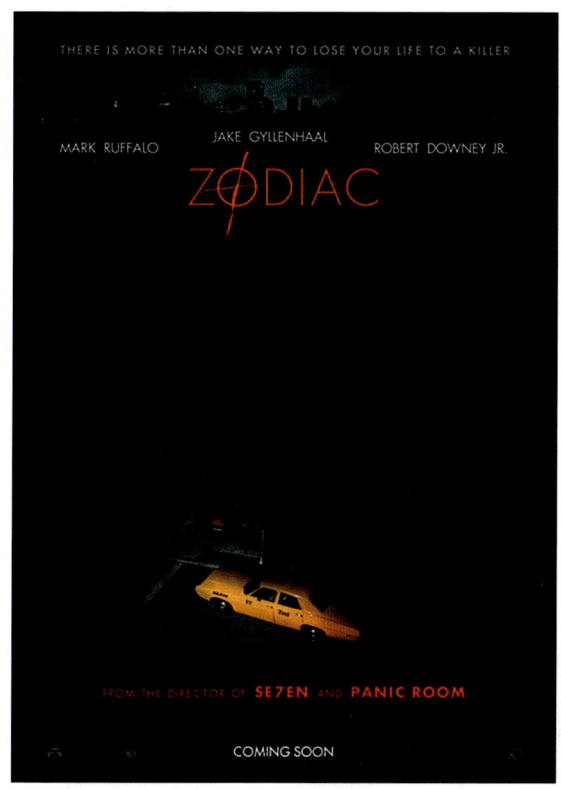

Zodiac

Zodiac – Die Spur des Killers
David Fincher, 2007
Jake Gyllenhaal

"The impression this movie leaves is profound:
Here is an artist who sees things whole."

New York Magazine

Spring, Summer, Fall, Winter ... and Spring

Frühling, Sommer, Herbst, Winter... und Frühling / Printemps, été, automne, hiver... et printemps
Kim Ki-duk, 2003
Seo Jae-kyeong, Ha Yeo-jin

Jane Fonda (1937)
Julie Delpy (1969)

Paramount Pictures presents a Dino De Laurentiis production, Jane Fonda in "Barbarella" starring John Phillip Law, Marcel Marceau, Special guest appearance David Hemmings as Dildano and with Ugo Tognazzi as Mark Hand, Produced by Dino De Laurentiis, Directed by Roger Vadim, From the bestseller "Barbarella" by Jean Claude Forest published by "Le Terrain Vague", Screenplay by Terry Southern, a Franco-Italian co-production, Dino De Laurentiis Cinematografica S.p.A. Marianne Productions, Panavision® Technicolor® A Paramount Pictures Re-Release

Barbarella

Roger Vadim, 1968
David Hemmings, Jane Fonda

"**There's a kind of Englishness there, a tradition of good manners and being attentive to other people that's also like a wall, and you feel you will never get in.**"

Ralph Fiennes

The Constant Gardener

Der ewige Gärtner
Fernando Meirelles, 2005
Ralph Fiennes

"I don't make films to serve the audience. I don't try to entice viewers to watch, understand, or even like my films — that's not my job."

Kim Ki-duk

Time

Kim Ki-duk, 2006
Park Ji-yeon

Miracle on 34th Street

Das Wunder von Manhattan /
Miracle sur la 34ème rue
Les Mayfield, 1994
Mara Wilson

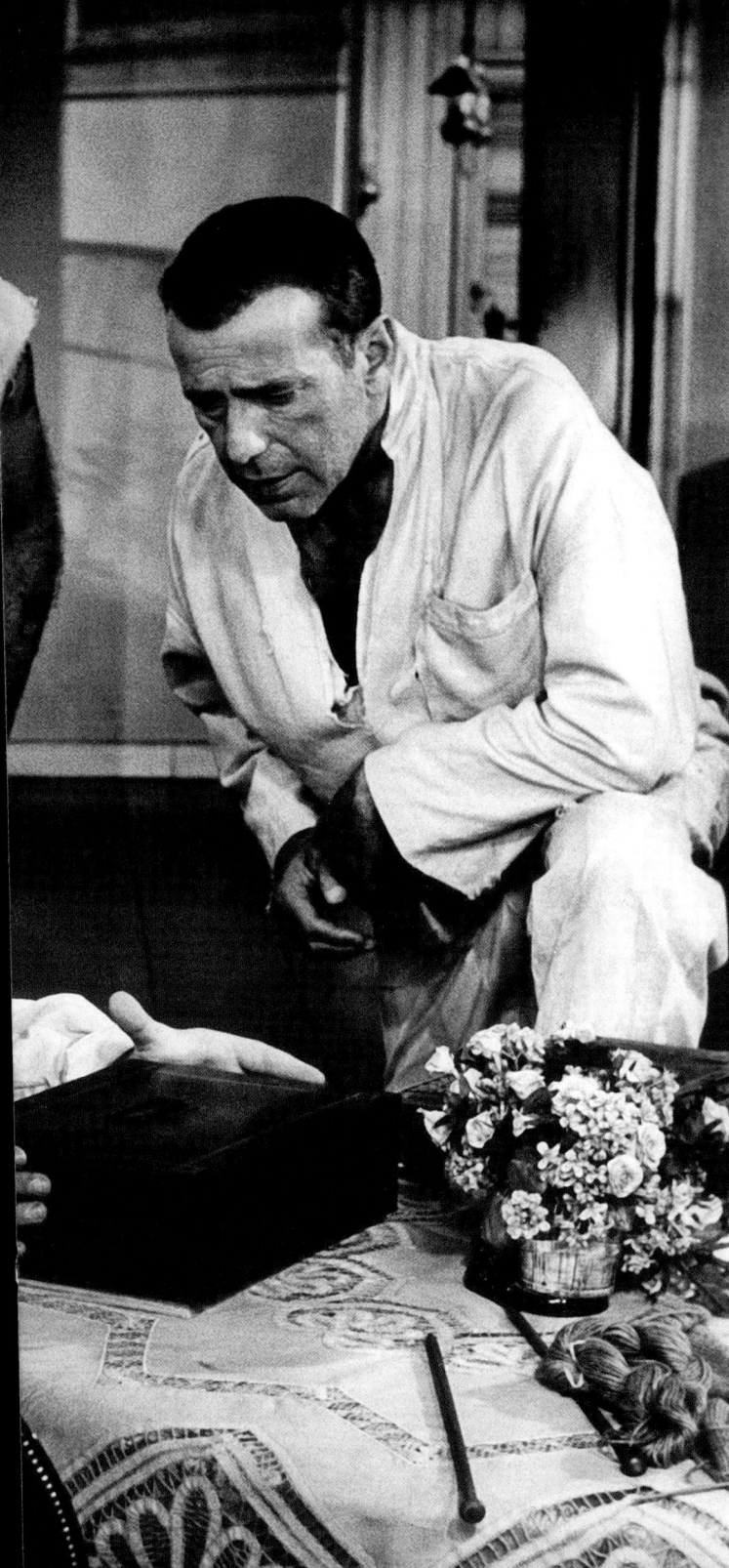

We're No Angels

Wir sind keine Engel / La Cuisine des anges
Michael Curtiz, 1955
Joan Bennett, Peter Ustinov,
Aldo Ray, Humphrey Bogart

Richard Widmark (1914)
Jared Leto (1971)

"Oh, games are important. They prepare a boy for the larger game of life, I'm told."

Earl of Dorincourt (Alec Guinness) to Lord Fauntleroy (Ricky Schroder)

Little Lord Fauntleroy

Der kleine Lord / Le Petit Lord Fauntleroy
Jack Gold, 1980
Ricky Schroder, Alec Guinness

Marlene Dietrich (1901)
Michel Piccoli (1925)

"A bizarre mixture of fairy tale and social-realist drama, snapping into sharpest focus when [Marlene Dietrich] performs the legendary 'Hot Voodoo' number while emerging from a gorilla-skin."

Time Out Film Guide

Blonde Venus

Blonde Vénus
Josef von Sternberg, 1932
Marlene Dietrich

F. W. Murnau (1888)
Hildegard Knef (1925)
Denzel Washington (1954)

"In *Curse of the Golden Flower* Mr. Zhang achieves a kind of operatic delirium, opening the floodgates of image and melodrama until the line between tragedy and black comedy is all but erased."

The New York Times

Curse of the Golden Flower

Der Fluch der goldenen Blume / La Cité interdite
Zhang Yimou, 2006
Gong Li

"I was really in good shape then, man. I was captain of the football team. And I wanted to be a war hero, man, I wanted to go out and kill for my country. And now, I'm here to tell you that I have killed for my country or whatever. And I don't feel good about it."

Luke Martin (Jon Voight)

Coming Home

Coming Home – Sie kehren heim / Le Retour
Hal Ashby, 1978
Jon Voight, Jane Fonda

Uzak

Nuri Bilge Ceylan, 2002
Emin Toprak

Anthony Hopkins (1937)
Ben Kingsley (1943)
Gong Li (1965)

"Filmed in a galaxy of colors."

The X from Outer Space

Itoka le monstre des galaxies
Kazui Nihonmatsu, 1967
Guilala

Index

Credits

Copyrights

© Aafa-Film AG Mar. 6 © Abbot Genser Sept. 19
© Abigayle Tarsches, Courtesy of New Line Productions
Jul. 24 © Altavista Films Feb. 6 © Amazonas
Oct. 12 © American Zoetrope May 1 © Arco
Film Mar. 5 © Arte Mar. 9 © Arthaus Filmverleih
Oct. 23, Nov. 24 © Atlas Film Jun. 24
© Bryanston Filmy Jul. 21 © Buena Vista
International Jan. 5, 27, Jul. 8, Oct. 10, Dec. 2
© Canal+ Jan. 25 © Carolco Pictures Apr. 15
© Centfox Feb. 1, Mar. 12, Apr. 19, 30, Jul. 18,
Aug. 31, Nov. 21, 25 © 1999 Matthew Barney,
photo: Chris Winget Dec. 10 © CIC Aug. 21
© Cineplex-Odeon Films Mar. 10 © Cineriz Sept. 29
© Cocinor May 22 © Columbia Filmverleih Aug. 2
© Columbia Pictures Jan. 10, Mar. 13, 28, Apr. 20,
29, May 18, Jul. 3, Sept. 21, 30, Oct. 16,
Nov. 6 © Columbia TriStar Jun. 15, Nov. 19
© Concorde Filmverleih Jun. 18, 20, Sept. 28,
Dec. 3 © Concorde-Castle Rock/Turner Mar. 19
© Constantin Film Feb. 22, Jul. 10, Aug. 28,
Nov. 15 © 1964 Danjaq, LLC, United Artists
Corporation. All rights reserved. Sept. 16 © 2006
Danjaq, LLC, United Artists Corporation and Columbia
Pictures Industries, Inc. All rights reserved. Mar. 2
© DCM Film Distribution May 3 © Deutsche Film
Hansa Feb. 25 © Deutsche Filmvertriebs GmbH (DFV)
Sept. 22 © Deutsche London-Film Verleih May 10
© Die Lupe Jun. 26 © Diego López Calvin Sept. 24
© Dimension Films Aug. 10 © DisCina Dec. 11
© Dreamworks Dec. 13 © Eagle-Lion Films Jul. 23
© East West Classics Sept. 12 © Estate of John R.
Hamilton Feb. 10 © Faces International Dec. 9
© Film Arts Guild Sept. 6 © Filmverlag der Autoren
Sept. 5 © Flach Film Feb. 17 © Fox 2000 Pictures
Oct. 28 © Fox Searchlight Pictures Jun. 23
© FOX-MGM Sept. 20 © Gramercy Pictures Aug. 17
© Hammer Film Productions Nov. 20 © Harris-

Kubrick Productions Dec. 12 © Herzog-Filmverleih
Jul. 1 © Highlight Film June 1 © Horizon Pictures
Jun. 22 © Howard Hughes Productions Feb. 26
© IFC Films Feb. 7 © Inter-Verleih Film-Gesellschaft
Oct. 22 © Internationale Filmallianz (IFA) Jul. 5
© Janus Films Jan. 23, April 9 © Jens Juncker-
Jensen Oct. 7 © Kinowelt Feb. 12, May 8
© Laurie Sparham, Courtesy of Serendipity Point Films
Sept. 10 © Les Films de Mon Oncle Feb. 16 © Les
Films du Carrosse Jun. 28 © Lumière Oct. 19
© Madman Entertainment Jul. 11 © Magnolia
Pictures Sept. 14 © Matt Nettheim Oct. 11
© Memfis Film Jan. 17 © Merie W. Wallace,
Courtesy of New Line Productions Aug. 4 © MGM
Jan. 8, 21, Feb. 28, Mar. 7, 12, 14, 22, Apr. 10,
18, May 15, June 2, 10, 16, 18, Sept. 18, Oct.
29, Nov. 2, 5, Dec. 8 © MGM/Filmways Mar. 24
© Michael James O'Brian, Courtesy Barbara Gladstone
Gallery Mar. 25 © Miramax Jan. 6, 29, Feb. 18,
Mar. 20, May 2 © Mirisch Company
June 8 © MK2 Diffusion Jun. 27, Oct. 30
© Moho Films Aug. 23 © Mongrel Media Dec.
28 © MPTV May 21 © Neue Constantin Film Mar.
17 © Neue Filmkunst Walter Kirchner Apr. 24
© New World Pictures May 9 © NewLineCinema
May 25 © O2 Filmes May 20 © Orion Pictures
Jun. 17 © Paola Ardizzoni, Emilio Pereda Sept. 15
© Paolo Pellion, Courtesy Galleria Francesca Kaufman
Jun. 30 © Paramount Pictures Jan. 11, 31, Feb.
13, 14, 20, Mar. 3, 16, Apr. 3, 4, 17, May 4, 23,
24, 30, Jun. 19, 21, Jul. 6, Aug. 12, 30, Oct.
15, 17, Nov. 10, 11, 14, 17, 23, Dec. 1, 4
© Pathé Cinéma Nov. 29 © Paul Gregory Productions
Oct. 14 © Philippe Halsman, Magnum, London/New
York/Paris Aug. 13 © PolyGram Jan. 7, Sept. 9
© Prisma Jul. 17 © Prokino Filmverleih Apr. 23,
Sept. 3, Nov. 22 © Raul Locatelli Nov. 26 © Red

Dragon Productions S.A. Feb. 5 © Revolution
Studios Apr. 13 © RKO Apr. 6, May 6, Jul. 7,
28, Aug. 7, 19, Oct. 24, Dec. 5 © Roadside
Attractions Jun. 12 © S.N. Prodis Nov. 8
© Saga Jan. 13 © Salem Jun. 11 © Sédig Mar. 8
© Senator Film Jan. 20, Aug. 27, Oct. 5
© Sheldon Reynolds Productions Sept. 11
© Sidus Pictures Jul. 4 © Slavia Film Nov. 9
© Sony Pictures Apr. 27, Oct. 31, Dec. 6 ©
Spike Jonze Jul. 2 © Svensk Filmindustri Nov. 13
© Tang Chak Sun Oct. 25 © Téléma Jan. 24
© Teresa Isasi Oct. 9 © The Archers Apr. 12
© The Weinstein Company Apr. 28 © Timebandits
Films Nov. 16 © TOBIS Film Jan. 2, Feb. 2,
Apr. 14, Jun. 14, 19, 31, Aug. 15, 22, Oct.
20 © Transcontinent May 17 © Twentieth Century
Fox Jan. 1, 22, Feb. 11, 19, 21, 27, Mar. 15,
18, 30, April 2, 21, May 14, 26, 27, Jun. 6, Jul.
21, 22, Aug. 9, 11, 16, 26, Sept. 4, 21, Jul. 15,
Oct. 1, 13, Nov. 18 © UFA Jan. 9, 16, May 11,
Apr. 26 © UIP Filmverleih Jan. 15, May 5, Jul. 9,
16, Aug. 1, 3, Sept. 27 © United Artists Jan. 19,
Feb. 24, Mar. 31, Apr. 16, 22, May 7, June 3,
7, Jul. 29, Sept. 26, Oct. 2, 4, 6, 17 © United
Artists, Mirisch Company, Pyramid Productions
Jun. 14 © Universal Jan. 4, Feb. 3, Apr. 1, 8,
11, 12, 25, Mar. 1, 26, 27, May 21, Aug. 6, 14,
18, 20, 24, 29, Sept. 23, Oct. 3 © Universum
Film Nov. 12 © Voltage Pictures Nov. 3 © Walt
Disney Pictures Jan. 12, Jun. 9, Sept. 1
© Warner Bros. Jan. 3, 14, 18, 26, 28, 30, Feb.
4, 8, 9, 15, 23, Mar. 4, 7, 21, April 5, May 16,
29, 31, Jun. 4, 5, 13, Jul. 13, 25, 26, Aug. 5,
8, 25, Sept. 7, Oct. 26, Nov. 7, 27 © Warner-
Columbia Filmverleih Sept. 25, Nov. 30 © William
Claxton Estate Jul. 20 © X Verleih Mar. 23

Image sources

All posters courtesy Heritage Auctions/HA.com
British Film Institute Stills, Posters and Designs,
London May 30, Jun. 25, 29, Jul. 30, Aug. 30,
Sept. 2, 8, 13, Oct. 27, Dec. 17
David Del Valle, The Del Valle Archives, Los Angeles
Mar. 11, 28, Apr. 11, Sept. 19, Oct. 8, Nov. 1,
28, Dec. 7
ddp images, Hamburg Jan. 1, 3, 4, 5, 6, 7, 8, 9,
12, 14, 18, 19, 20, 21, 22, 23, 24, 25, 26, 27,
28, 29, Feb. 2, 3, 4, 9, 11, 12, 13, 15, 17, 18,

19, 21, 22, 23, 24, 25, 27, 28, Mar. 2, 4, 5, 6, 9,
12, 14, 15, 17, 18, 19, 20, 23, 26, 29, 31, Apr.
1, 3, 4, 9, 10, 14, 16, 17, 18, 20, 21, 22, 23, 24,
25, 26, 28, 29, May 2, 3, 4, 5, 6, 7, 8, 10, 11,
12, 14, 15, 18, 22, 26, 27, 29, 31, Jun. 1, 2, 3,
6, 10, 12, 13, 14, 15, 16, 17, 18, 19, 20, 23, 24,
26, 27, Jul. 1, 3, 5, 6, 7, 8, 9, 10, 13, 14, 15,
16, 17, 21, 22, 26, 27, 28, 31, Aug. 1, 2, 3, 5,
6, 8, 9, 14, 15, 16, 17, 18, 21, 22, 24, 26, 27,
28, Sep. 3, 5, 6, 7, 9, 16, 17, 18, 20, 21, 22, 25,

26, 27, 28, 29, 30, Oct. 1, 2, 4, 5, 6, 10, 13, 18,
20, 22, 23, 24, 30, Nov. 5, 8, 9, 10, 11, 14, 15,
16, 17, 18, 19, 22, 23, 24, 27, 30, Dec. 1, 2, 3,
4, 5, 6, 8, 9, 11, 16, 18, 19, 20, 21, 22, 23, 24,
27, 29, 31
The Kobal Collection, London/New York Mar. 11, 30,
Apr. 2, 6, May 9, 23, Sept. 19, Oct. 8, Nov. 28,
Dec. 7, 11, 25

To stay informed about upcoming TASCHEN titles, please request our magazine at www.taschen.com/magazine or write to TASCHEN, Hohenzollernring 53, D-50672 Cologne, Germany; contact@taschen.com. We will be happy to send you a free copy of our magazine, which is filled with information about all of our books.

FRONT COVER Liza Minnelli in *Cabaret* by Bob Fosse, 1972

BACK COVER Peter Lorre in *M / M – Eine Stadt sucht einen Mörder / M le maudit* by Fritz Lang, 1931

FRONTISPIECE Marilyn Monroe in *The Seven Year Itch / Das verflixte 7. Jahr / Sept ans de réflexion* by Billy Wilder, 1979

PAGE 734 Azharuddin Mohammed Ismail and Ayush Mahesh Khedekar in *Slumdog Millionaire / Slumdog Millionär / Le Pouilleux millionnaire* by Danny Boyle, 2008

PAGE 743 Slim Pickens in *Dr. Strangelove or: How I Learned to Stop Worrying and Love the Bomb / Dr. Seltsam, oder wie ich lernte, die Bombe zu lieben / Docteur Folamour ou : comment j'ai appris à ne plus m'en faire et à aimer la bombe* by Stanley Kubrick, 1964

EDITORIAL COORDINATION Florian Kobler, Martin Holz and Jonas Scheler, Cologne
ART DIRECTION Josh Baker, Los Angeles
DESIGN Jessica Trujillo, Los Angeles
PRODUCTION Daniela Schädlich, Cologne

© 2013 TASCHEN GmbH
Hohenzollernring 53, D–50672 Köln
www.taschen.com

Printed in China

ISBN 978-3-8365-3862-6